Basic Quiltmaking Techniques

for Strip Piecing

Paulette Peters

Martingale
& C O M P A N Y
Bothell, Washington

Credits

Technical Editor . . . . Christine Barnes
Design and Production Manager . . Cheryl Stevenson
Text Designer . . . . Kay Green
Cover Designer . . . . Magrit Baurecht
Copy Editor . . . . Liz McGehee
Illustrator . . . . Laurel Strand
Photographer . . . . Brent Kane

Basic Quiltmaking Techniques for Strip Piecing
© 1998 by Paulette Peters

Martingale
& COMPANY

Martingale & Company
PO Box 118
Bothell, WA 98041-0118 USA

Printed in the United States of America
03 02 01 00 99   6 5 4 3

The information in this book is presented in good faith, but no warranty is given nor results guaranteed. Since Martingale & Company has no control over choice of materials or procedures, it assumes no responsibility for the use of this information.

Dedication

This book is dedicated to beginning quiltmakers. Your excitement retrieves the sense of wonder that all of us felt at the beginning. May you have many creative experiences, and may strip piecing contribute to your successful projects.

Acknowledgments

Thanks to Carol Doak for her book, *Your First Quilt Book (or it should be!),* for her wise advice, and for including me in her team. Thanks to Ursula Reikes at Martingale & Company for the opportunity to work with her, for her professional expertise, and for those sudden trips to the fabric store.

Library of Congress Cataloging-in Publication Data
Peters, Paulette,
    Basic quiltmaking techniques for strip piecing
    / Paulette Peters.
       p. cm.
    Includes bibliographical references.
    ISBN 1-56477-232-2
    1. Strip quilting—Patterns. 2. Patchwork—
    Patterns. I. Title.
TT835.P449127 1998
746.46'041—dc21   98-20252
                   CIP

MISSION STATEMENT

WE ARE DEDICATED TO PROVIDING QUALITY PRODUCTS AND SERVICE BY WORKING TOGETHER TO INSPIRE CREATIVITY AND TO ENRICH THE LIVES WE TOUCH.

Table of Contents

Foreword

Basic Quiltmaking Techniques for Strip Piecing is our second book in the Basic Quiltmaking Techniques series. This series is designed to take you beyond the basic quiltmaking skills you learned in *Your First Quilt Book (or it should be!)* and open new horizons to additional techniques. You will find the same comfortable format and conversational text in this book that you came to enjoy and appreciate in *Your First Quilt Book*. The basic quiltmaking information in that book will not be repeated here, except as it relates to strip-piecing techniques, so you can focus on these new avenues.

Strip piecing is a wonderful technique for quilters of all skill levels. Many traditional patchwork blocks that were worked piece by piece years ago can now be made easily, accurately, and with lightning speed using rotary cutters and rotary rulers.

Paulette Peters is an accomplished quiltmaker and teacher. Her enthusiasm for this wonderful technique is infectious, and I have no doubt she will have you strip piecing with ease in no time. Paulette takes you beyond the basics. You will learn which patchwork block designs are ideal candidates for strip-piecing techniques

and how to dissect designs into strip-piecing opportunities. Along the way, she shares her secrets and tips for strip-piecing success.

Paulette shows you how to calculate the strips and units needed to complete the blocks. You will learn two quick and accurate methods for sewing strips of fabric together to make bias squares—important design elements in many traditional blocks.

You'll practice what you learn right away because Paulette has designed eight delightful beginner projects you can make using strip-piecing methods. I am sure you will find several to make for yourself, friends, and family. Her step-by-step instructions and illustrations make it seem so quick and easy!

Just as the basic quiltmaking information in *Your First Quilt Book* laid the foundation for quiltmaking skills, the techniques you learn in *Basic Quiltmaking Techniques for Strip Piecing* will provide you with strip-piecing skills you can use again and again in future patchwork projects.

So sit back, cozy up in a comfortable chair, and discover the wonderful world of strip piecing.

Carol Doak

Introduction

This book is designed for beginning quiltmakers. It complements *Your First Quilt Book (or it should be!)* by Carol Doak and introduces strip piecing, a technique that will add to the success and pleasure of your patchwork projects. All of the projects are designed for rotary cutting and machine piecing.

Strip piecing is a simple technique: You cut strips of fabric, sew them together, cut new shapes or segments, and sew again. Suddenly, it's a quilt! Strip piecing is quick, accurate, and fun. With a little experience, you'll soon be looking for ways to "sew first and cut later" in every patchwork project you plan to make.

Paulette Peters

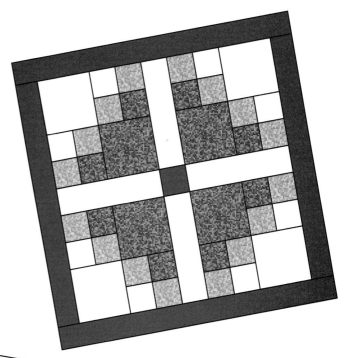

How to Use This Book

If you have read *Your First Quilt Book*, you are already familiar with many of the basic quiltmaking techniques. If you need more help with the quiltmaking process, you will most likely find it in this excellent resource.

In this book, begin at the beginning, with the "Strip-Piecing Glossary" (opposite) and "Choosing Fabrics" (page 8). Each project has tips for choosing a pleasing combination of fabrics. Also check out the list of "Tools" (page 10). Rotary-cutting tools are especially helpful for strip piecing.

Next, read "Strip-Piecing Principles" (page 12) and "Strip-Piecing Techniques, Step by Step" (page 14) to get acquainted with the strip-piecing process. Bias squares are an important design element, and they are simple to make using strip-piecing techniques (page 20).

The materials lists specify 44"-wide fabric, but the instructions assume a minimum of 42" of usable width to allow for shrinkage. If your fabric has more than 42" of usable width, you may have a little fabric left over. If it has less, you may need to cut an extra strip or piece.

Once you're familiar with the fundamentals, select a project and read the directions carefully. Then it's off to the fabric store for fabric and tools.

Really use this book—mark it up! Write your color choices next to mine in the color key, or tape small fabric scraps to the page. Then you can see at a glance which fabric goes where.

As you read, you will find three important symbols:

Tip: A helpful hint to make the process easier. Read these right away.

Alert: This symbol tells you to watch for something that might cause a problem. Your guardian angel will help you avoid potential snags.

Down the Road: This box provides information for future quiltmaking projects. You can refer to it when you are ready to tackle more complex projects.

Strip-Piecing Glossary

Bias grain: The grain line that runs at a 45° angle to the selvage. The bias grain is the stretchiest part of the fabric.

Bias square: A square made up of two triangles sewn together on their long sides. See **Half-square triangles.**

Block: A unit created by sewing patches together. This is the basic design element in pieced quilts.

Chain piecing: The technique of sewing patches consecutively without cutting the thread between them. Also known as *fast feeding*.

Crosscuts: See **Segments.**

Dog ears: Fabric points that appear when seam allowances are pressed to one side. Trim dog ears to reduce bulk.

Fat quarter: Precut fabric pieces that measure 18" x 22", rather than 9" across the width of the bolt. This cut gives quilters more usable fabric.

Half-square triangles: Triangles created from a square cut once diagonally from corner to corner. The straight grain is on the short sides of the triangle.

Lattice: See **Sashing.**

Quarter-square triangles: Triangles created from a square cut twice diagonally from corner to corner. The straight grain is on the long side of the triangles.

Rotary cutter: A tool with a round razorlike blade (like a pizza cutter). Expect a long and loving relationship.

Sashing: Strips of fabric sewn between the blocks. Also known as *lattice*.

Seam allowance: Extra fabric beyond the sewing line that allows you to join patchwork pieces. The standard seam allowance for patchwork is ¼" on all sides of each shape.

Segments: Pieces cut from a strip set into specified widths to form new units, much like slices of bread cut from a loaf. Also known as *crosscuts*.

Selvage: The tightly woven lengthwise edge of fabric. Cut the selvage off before cutting your patchwork pieces.

Squaring up: Pressing a block to the correct size and shape or trimming it (only if necessary).

Straight grain: The grain line that runs vertically, parallel to the selvage (lengthwise grain), or horizontally, from selvage to selvage (crosswise grain).

Strata: See **Strip set.**

Strip piecing: The process of sewing strips of fabric together, cutting them into segments, and re-sewing them one or more times to create patchwork.

Strips: Pieces of fabric cut across the width of the fabric, from selvage to selvage, at specified widths. Strips are straight and true. They will be shorter if you use fat quarters.

Strip set: A panel of fabric strips sewn together on the long edges. Also known as *strata*.

Choosing Fabrics
(or, "How Do I Know Which Bolts Will Work?")

Selecting fabrics is perhaps the most exciting and challenging aspect of quiltmaking. Following are a few guidelines to help you when you are standing before a wall of fabric in the quilt shop. Don't be afraid to pull out lots of bolts, stack them on the floor or a table, and stand back to study the effect. Quilt shop owners understand a quilter's need to stroke the fabric, and they don't mind a mess, especially if you offer to put away your "toys" when you finish playing.

Fiber Content

Quilters love 100% cotton fabric, for good reason. All-cotton fabric is the right weight and texture for quilting. The colors and patterns are beautiful, and it's easy to cut, stitch, and press all-cotton fabric. Cotton fabrics are also dependable, except for occasional fading or bleeding (excess dye that stains another fabric during washing).

You can use fabric with some polyester content, but the results are unpredictable. The directional sheen of cotton-polyester blends makes cutting more difficult because you must cut each piece on the same grain. These blends don't press into flat, crisp seams, and it is difficult to ease a larger piece to a smaller one without lots of crinkles.

Heavy-weight cotton fabric, used for upholstery or draperies, can add interest to a quilt, but it's difficult to handle with ¼" seams. Decorator fabrics are a great resource for experienced quilters.

Fading and Bleeding

You can take steps to minimize the problems of fading and bleeding. Light causes the most fading. Think about how your quilt will be used and, if possible, avoid placing it in direct sunlight or near a window. If you're planning to hang your quilt in a light place, look for light-colored fabric; any fading that occurs will be less noticeable. Navy blue, black, some browns, and dark green are fading champions. Protect them from the light.

Bleeding is the "white-sweater-washed-with-a-red-sock" experience—a very distressing problem for a quiltmaker. Check for bleeding before you cut a fabric. If a fabric is dark, feels stiff, or smells as though it contains lots of chemicals, wash it. Then wash it again with a scrap of white fabric. If the white fabric shows any color, wash the dark fabric again. If the fabric continues to bleed, don't use it in your quilt.

Color

As you choose your fabrics, consider the following aspects of color and design.

Contrast

When it comes to quiltmaking, color isn't as important as value (the lightness or darkness of a fabric). Quilters cut up fabric and sew it back together to create a patchwork design. If the values of the fabrics are too similar, the pieces will blend and you won't see the design.

How do you know if the values have enough contrast? Suppose you are planning to use a rose and a green fabric in a quilt block. To check for value contrast, lay the two fabrics side by side and step back five feet. Or, squint at the fabric. Do you see a distinct difference between the two? A fabric that reads "medium rose" by itself and a fabric that reads "dark green" by itself may both look medium when placed side by side.

To "read" a fabric, ask yourself, How does it look from a distance? Which color is dominant? Is it light, medium, or dark? The little pink flowers you see up close aren't important, but the large white areas may show from across the room.

Visual Texture

Beginning quilters often select fabrics that look similar in design, such as several small florals, several tone-on-tone prints from the same manufacturer, or the same print in different colors. This approach is easy but less interesting than mixing lots of wonderful textures and patterns.

You can mix texture and pattern by considering the scale and line of your potential fabrics. For example, try a large floral print with a small floral print that has similar colors. Then, add a print with swirly lines, but no flowers. These prints are all soft-lined and natural. Now add a plaid, stripe, or geometric. These patterns balance the swirls and create even more visual interest. When it comes to combining texture and pattern, be adventurous.

Use care when choosing fabrics with a directional pattern, such as a plaid, stripe, or floral motif with strong design lines. Strip piecing gives you less control over the way the design appears in the finished piece because you may be turning the sewn units in different directions. The effect can be charming and spontaneous, but it may also look like careless piecing. If you do fall in love with a directional fabric, you can use it in strip piecing with a little planning. See the "Table Runner" on page 47.

Finding a Great Color Group

Clues to color choices are all around us. Train your eye to really look at the colors you see. If the person in front of you in church is wearing a wonderful sweater, look carefully at the colors. Wouldn't that plum, teal, and taupe be great in a quilt? Run to the quilt shop with that combination in mind.

Consider your living room furniture and accessories. You might pick up some of the colors in your sofa for a quilt. Accessories can give you clues for accent colors.

Look out the window. Nature is a great inspiration. Take snapshots of your garden and go to the quilt shop with a picture of zinnias, daisies, and delphiniums—great quilt colors! And don't miss the color choices in famous paintings; a museum is a terrific place for inspiration.

In other words, be on a constant search for great color groups. Look at magazines, books, and any other visual resources. Keep a notebook with clippings of pleasing color combinations.

Of course, one of the easiest methods for finding a color group is to select a "master" fabric with several colors in it. Then use those colors to help you choose other fabrics. *Caution:* Don't try to match the colors in a master fabric exactly. I've seen quilters freeze if the green doesn't exactly match the tiny leaf in a floral print. Look at the group of fabrics from a polite distance and see if it's pleasing. How does it read? Is it overmatched? Does it have just a little bit of color surprise? When you make your color decisions, take a broad perspective.

You'll find color suggestions with each project, under "Choosing Fabrics." Refer to *Your First Quilt Book* for more help with fabric choices.

If you like a fabric on the bolt, you'll probably like it in your quilt. Be sure to look at a small portion to see how it will work best in your block.

Tools

Good tools are the key to success in quilt-making. You'll also enjoy the process more if you have the right tools. Refer to *Your First Quilt Book* for a complete list of quiltmaking tools. The following tools are especially helpful for strip piecing.

Rotary cutter. Buy the medium-size (45mm) rotary cutter. The smaller size is good for curves, but it won't cut through the layers you need for strip piecing. Buy extra blades so you can replace the original blade as soon as it gets dull.

Dull blades make for frustrated quilters. Replace the blade as soon as it leaves little uncut threads on your strips. Carefully remove the parts of the cutter and lay them down in the order you take them off. Replace the blade, remove lint from the pieces, and reassemble. The blade should roll as you push the cutter along the mat. If it doesn't, loosen the screw slightly. If your cutter doesn't have an automatic shield, place a drop of sewing-machine oil on the parts that slide to make opening and closing easier.

Respect your rotary cutter. Unless you plan to wear steel gloves in your work space, get in the habit of closing the rotary cutter every time you set it down. Of course, always keep it out of the reach of children.

Cutting mat. Use a mat with a grid for lining up your fabric. Buy the largest size (at least 18" x 24") you can fit on your cutting surface. Protect your mat from heat and bending. Store it flat, if possible, and never leave it in a hot car. Many curled mats come to class—and never recover their shape.

Rotary rulers. Many rulers are available, and quilters like to play the game of who can collect the most rulers. They must be heavy acrylic and thick enough to guide the cutter without chipping. The following is a list of rulers you need for strip piecing, in order of importance, from "must-have" to "add-to-your-birthday-list."

• A 24" ruler marked in ¼" increments. Use this ruler to cut strips across the width of the fabric. I prefer one *without* a lip that hooks over the mat.

• An 8" square ruler with a right-angle mark. My favorite is the Bias Square® from Martingale & Company. This ruler is convenient for cutting bias squares and segments from strip sets.

When you want to add to your ruler collection, consider these:

• A large square ruler, 12" to 16", for cutting large squares

• A 14" ruler to cut strips from folded fabric and carry to workshops

• A 4" square ruler for small pieces

Sandpaper tabs. Place these little stick-on pieces of sandpaper on the underside of your rotary rulers. They help the ruler grab the fabric and keep it from slipping.

Strip piecing doesn't require a special sewing machine or fancy accessories. However, a number of basic accessories will help make your work easy and accurate.

Seam guide. Look in your box of attachments for a seam guide. Set it at ¼" to give your fabric strips a ridge to push against as you sew. This accessory helps you sew straight seams on long strips.

Patchwork foot. If your machine has a presser foot with a ¼" edge on it, use it. If not, add the foot to your wish list.

Walking foot. A walking foot isn't necessary for piecing, but you'll want it when you begin to machine quilt straight lines. A walking foot is also great for sewing on bindings.

Needles. Use a sharp needle, size 70/10 or 80/12, for piecing.

Thread. Choose a good-quality, medium-weight thread that doesn't leave fuzz in the machine. Use a neutral color, such as gray or beige, for most piecing. If you're piecing a very dark and a very light fabric together, use thread that matches the dark.

Take care of your machine—it's your best friend. Each time you start a new project, clean and oil the machine, put in a new needle, and give the machine a kiss. Clean out the lint every time you change the bobbin. You'll both be happier and perform better. Have your machine serviced on a regular basis—it can do wonders for your tension. Most dealers offer regular maintenance check-ups.

Seam ripper (or un-sewer). A seam ripper is an essential tool for strip piecing. Use it as an extra finger to hold small pieces in place as you feed them into the machine. And of course, "She who sews shall also un-sew." All quilters need to rip out and re-sew a seam occasionally. Choose a seam ripper with a fine point and replace it regularly. Seam rippers get dull, just like scissors.

To quickly remove a seam, work on the bobbin side of the seam. Snip every third or fourth stitch along the length of the seam. Turn the piece over and pull the top thread. This method is quick, but messy; you'll need to brush off the thread wisps.

Iron and accessories. Use the flattest padding you can find for your ironing board. A firm surface helps to make crisp seams that are so necessary for strip sets.

A dry iron, set on cotton, works best because steam irons, especially those with an automatic shut-off, can spit onto your fabric at the wrong moment.

Keep a spray bottle next to the ironing board to mist seams and press them dry.

If a fabric is soft and stretchy, try spraying it with spray sizing, available at many grocery stores. Sizing firms up the fabric, but isn't as heavy as spray starch.

Strip-Piecing Principles

The strip-piecing concept is simple: Handle as few small pieces as possible when you piece patchwork blocks. Why cut many little squares, pick up each one, match it to another square, and then sew them together? The fewer pieces you need to handle, the more accurate and efficient you'll be.

The strip-piecing process is also simple: You cut strips of fabric, sew them together, cut segments, and sew them together. Patterns that adapt well to strip piecing are Four Patch, Nine Patch, Puss-in-the-Corner, and Rail Fence. These blocks all have straight lines connecting the pieces, and they fit on a grid of squares.

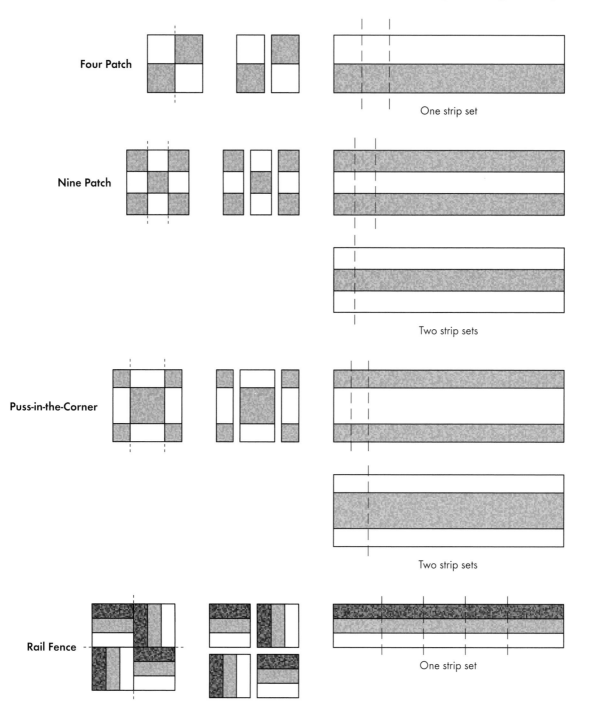

Patterns that radiate from the center, such as an Eight-Pointed Star, cannot be strip pieced. However, you can adapt the pattern for strip piecing.

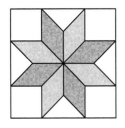

Eight-pointed star

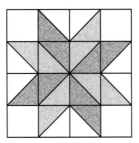

Eight-pointed star with strip-pieced bias squares

You'll find more information on patchwork block designs in *Your First Quilt Book*.

Grain Lines

Fabric grain is important in strip piecing because it dictates how you cut the strips. The goal in strip piecing is to have a stable edge on each quilt block and to avoid stretchy bias edges. Strips for squares and rectangles are almost always cut on the crosswise grain, from selvage to selvage. Strips from fat quarters are also cut on the crosswise grain (the 22"-long edge) for the longest strips. Strips for bias squares or triangles are cut on the diagonal grain, at a 45° angle to the straight grain. See "Making Bias Squares" on page 20.

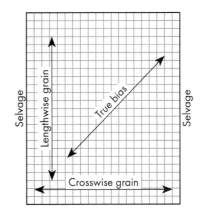

Strip-Piecing Techniques, Step by Step

To use strip-piecing techniques, a block or other element must have straight lines connecting the pieces and fit on a grid of squares.

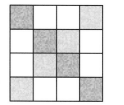 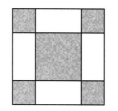

Following are the four steps in the strip-piecing process. Careful work at all stages will make your stitching a breeze.

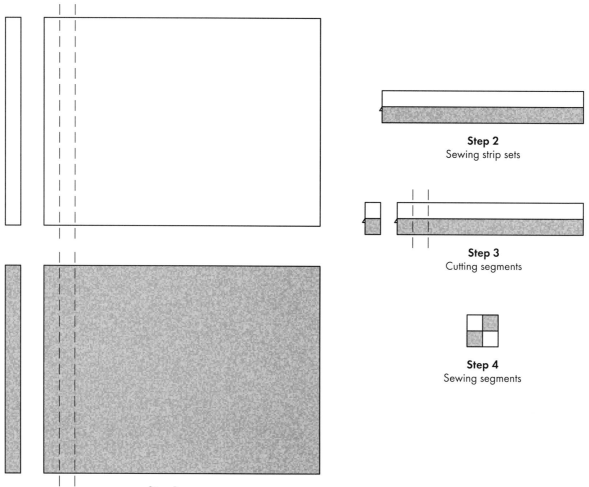

Step 2
Sewing strip sets

Step 3
Cutting segments

Step 4
Sewing segments

Step 1
Cutting strips

Step 1: Cutting Strips

Accurate strip-pieced blocks start with carefully cut strips. Follow these simple steps for cutting your strips.

1. Fold the fabric lengthwise by laying one selvage on a horizontal line of your cutting mat and bringing the other selvage up to meet it. Usually, the cut end doesn't line up.

If you see a V-shape between the selvages, refold the fabric. A V-shape on the cut end is fine.

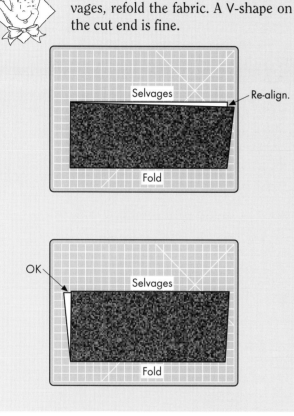

2. Lay the fold along a horizontal line on your mat. Always work from the fold, not the selvage edge. Align your rotary ruler on a horizontal and vertical line, making sure the vertical line you select will allow you to cut both layers of fabric. Check the horizontal and vertical positions of your ruler. Stabilize the ruler with your little finger and push the rotary cutter away from you to make the first cut and square off the fabric. Discard the trimmed edge. Following are illustrations for both right-handed and left-handed cutting.

Right-handed

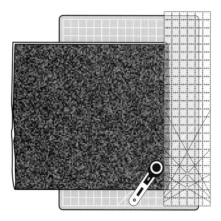

Left-handed

3. Align the appropriate markings on your ruler (such as the 2" marks for a 2"-wide strip) with the clean-cut edge. Check to make sure that a horizontal line on the ruler is aligned with the fold. Also check to see that the vertical line on the ruler is precisely even with the cut edge. Cut.

Right-handed

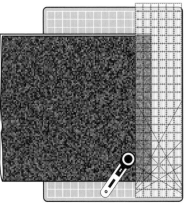

Left-handed

4. Open the first strip to see if it is straight; if not, refold the fabric, aligning the selvages, and square off the fabric again.

Leave the folded fabric in position while cutting your strips. Moving the fabric shifts the cut end.

If you cut a crooked strip, cut it in half, and use the two pieces. The grain won't be exactly true, but sewing the strips to other strips will stabilize them.

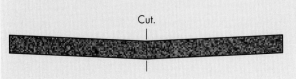
Cut.

Hints for Successful Rotary Cutting

• Use the marked grid on your mat for aligning the fabric fold and the ruler, and for cutting right angles. Do not use the grid for measuring.

• Check the ruler at two places before cutting. Be sure the ruler is lined up both horizontally and vertically with the fabric. Use the following checklist for perfect cutting:

  a. Fabric fold aligned with horizontal line on mat

  b. Vertical line on ruler aligned with clean-cut edge and parallel to a vertical line on mat

  c. Horizontal line on ruler aligned with fabric fold

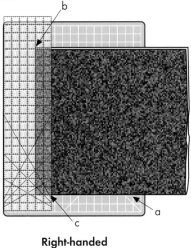

Right-handed

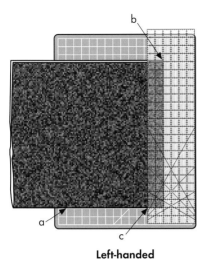

Left-handed

• After cutting three or four strips, refold and recut if necessary. The pressure of the cutter pushes the fabric slightly out of line, causing misshapen strips.

• Double-check the desired width on the ruler each time you cut, or mark the ruler with a piece of masking tape. Remember the adage: Measure twice, cut once.

 Remove masking tape when you finish your project; tape permanently adheres to rotary rulers.

Handling and Storing Strips

Cut edges can ravel or become fuzzy if handled too much. Leave the strips folded and lying flat until you're ready to sew. Keep leftover strips in a box or flat basket, sorted by width. They're great for future projects. It's a quilting legend that fabric strips multiply if left unattended; quilters usually cut more than needed.

Step 2: Sewing Strip Sets

Once you've cut your strips, you're ready to sew them into strip sets.

Sewing an Accurate 1/4"-wide Seam Allowance

Sew strips in pairs along the cut edges with a straight, 1/4"-wide seam allowance. The best five minutes you'll ever spend are those checking the seam allowance on your sewing machine. Follow these steps:

1. Place a rotary ruler under the presser foot.
2. Gently drop the needle onto the 1/4" line on the right edge of the ruler.
3. Lower the presser foot to hold the ruler in place.
4. Straighten the ruler so it is aligned with the edge of the machine.
5. Place several layers of masking tape along the right edge of the ruler.

Sew a sample seam, using the seam guide, and measure from the seam line to the cut edge. It should be exactly 1/4" wide. Refer to *Your First Quilt Book* for further information.

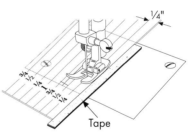

Tape

 Accurate seam allowances are essential for precision strip piecing. If the seams on your strip sets are too narrow, the cut segments will be too long. If your seams are too wide, the cut segments will be too short.

| Accurate seam allowances | Seam allowances too narrow | Seam allowances too wide |

To join two strips, match the selvage ends; then hold your finger between the two strips, like the reins on a horse, and align them as you sew. You'll soon be driving 100 miles per hour in your stocking feet and sewing perfectly straight seams.

 Not all fabrics are the same width, so start sewing at the selvage each time you add a strip, and you will have one straight end for measuring and cutting segments.

Selvages

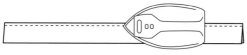

Pressing the Strip Sets

1. Press the stitches from the wrong side of the fabric to set them.

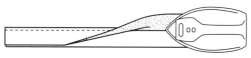

Press the stitching.

2. Lift the top strip and gently press it outward, keeping the seam crisp and flat. Make sure the strip pair is straight, and press without distorting it into a curve.

Press the seam.

3. Press each pair of strips before adding another strip to the set.

 Usually, you press the seam allowances toward the dark fabric to prevent the dark seam allowance from showing through to the right side. In some projects, however, it may be necessary to press toward the lighter fabric to match seam intersections. Follow the pressing directions and arrows in each project and check the front of the strip set as you go to see if the dark seam allowances show. If so, trim them slightly.

Step 3: Cutting Segments

Once your strip sets are pressed flat and straight, you're ready to crosscut them into segments.

1. Lay the strip on the cutting mat and align one long edge with a horizontal grid line on the mat.
2. Align the ruler along a vertical grid line on the mat and trim the rough selvage edge. (Never use the selvage in any project.)

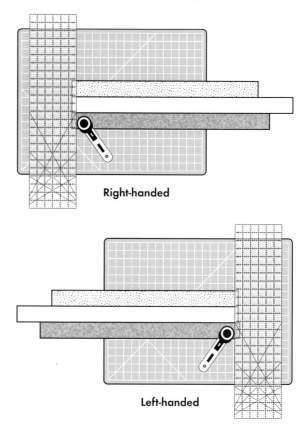

Right-handed

Left-handed

3. Align the appropriate markings on your ruler (such as the 2" marks for a 2"-wide segment) with the clean-cut edge. Check to see that the vertical line on the ruler is precisely even with the cut edge of the strip set. Cut the segments.

Refer to the illustration below and use the following checklist for perfect cutting:

a. Edge of strip set aligned with horizontal line on mat
b. Vertical line on ruler aligned with clean-cut edge and parallel to vertical line on mat
c. Horizontal line on ruler aligned with one seam on strip set

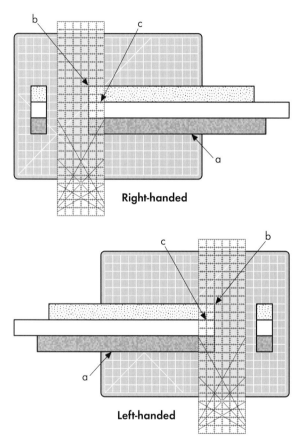

Right-handed

Left-handed

If the seam allowances on the strip sets have been pressed in opposite directions, you can cut two layers of segments at one time. Lay one strip set right side up and the other strip set right side down, nestling the seams together. Run your finger along the seams, smoothing them so

they interlock. Cut the segment and leave the pairs together, ready for sewing. "Four Patch Pillow" (page 42) and "Hot Squares" (page 56) use this technique.

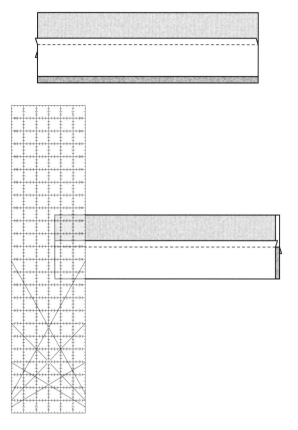

Step 4: Sewing Segments

Chain-sew the segments, making sure that the seams interlock.

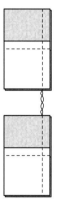

Making Bias Squares

A square made up of two triangles of different fabric is known as a bias square. You'll find this design element in many traditional quilt blocks. Strip piecing is an accurate method for making bias squares.

Bias square

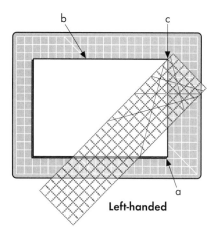

Left-handed

You begin by cutting strips on the bias and sewing them together. Then you cut squares to the size required for the project, aligning the diagonal line on the Bias Square ruler with the seam line on the strip set. The outer edges of the bias square are on the straight grain, and the diagonal seam, which is on the bias, is crisp and straight.

1. For easier handling, cut the fabric into pieces no longer than 18" on the lengthwise grain. To make fewer bias squares, start with a square of each fabric. Layer the two fabrics, right sides together, and press to adhere them.

2. Make a clean-cut edge on the crosswise grain, just as if you were preparing to cut a straight strip.

3. Lay the clean-cut edge on a horizontal line on the mat, with the selvage edge on a vertical line. Place the 45°-angle line of the ruler on the vertical edge of the fabric. Make a diagonal cut. Use the following checklist for perfect cutting:
   a. Selvage on vertical mat line
   b. Clean-cut edge on horizontal mat line
   c. 45° ruler line on vertical edge of fabric

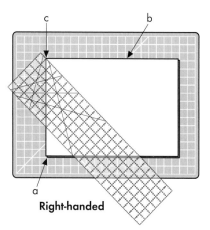

Right-handed

4. Cut the diagonal strips at the specified width. Leave the strip pairs together.

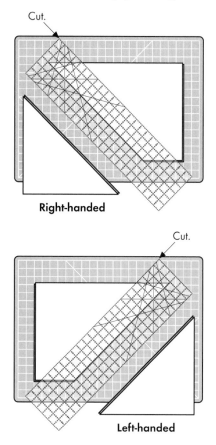

Right-handed

Left-handed

Note: These strips have bias edges; be careful not to stretch them. Pin the strips every few inches to hold them together while you sew.

Make bias squares from the strips, using either of the following methods:

Method 1

1. Sew both edges of each strip pair, using a ¼"-wide seam allowance.
2. Press the strips to set the stitches.
3. Position a Bias Square ruler with the diagonal line on the seam line and the desired cut size of the bias square (the finished size plus ½") on the straight grain. Move the ruler from side to side to cut triangles from each side of the strip.

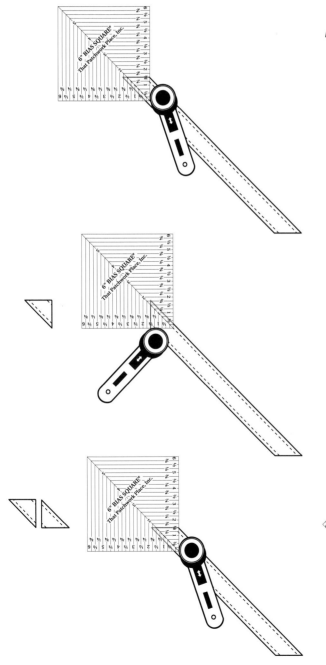

4. Undo the few stitches in the point. Press the seams toward the dark fabric and trim the dog ears.

Mark the lines on the ruler with masking tape.

Method 2

1. Sew along one edge of each strip pair, using a ¼"-wide seam allowance.
2. Press the strips to set the stitches. Press the seam toward the dark fabric. A V-shape will form at one end of the bias strip set.
3. Position a Bias Square ruler with the diagonal line on the seam line and the desired measurement at the point of the V. Cut the upper edges. Turn each piece and cut the remaining two edges to make a bias square. Continue cutting bias squares. Use the waste triangles for other projects

If you are making a project that doesn't specify the cut width of the bias strips for bias squares, follow these steps:

1. Divide the finished size of the bias square you want to make by 1.414. Add ⅝" (.625) for seam allowances to determine the cut width of the bias strips. If, for example, you want to make bias squares that measure 3" x 3" finished, you must cut bias strips 2¾" wide (3" ÷ 1.414 = 2.12, or 2⅛", + ⅝" = 2¾").

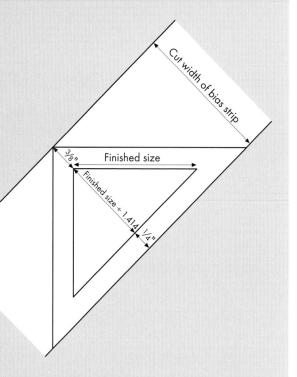

2. Add ½" to the finished size of the bias square to determine the cut size (3" + ½" = 3½").

Calculating Strip Width and Length

Once you understand the basics of strip piecing, you are free to choose your own block sizes and setting designs. You can still work quickly and efficiently, whether you apply strip-piecing techniques to your own designs or look for opportunities to use them in traditional quilt blocks.

As you work through the projects in this book, you may want to change the size of the block or adapt another block to these settings. Following are instructions for making changes.

• Cut each strip as wide as the finished width of the piece in the block, plus ½" for seam allowances (¼" on each edge).

• Cut each segment as wide as the finished width of the piece in the block, plus ½" for seam allowances.

• Each strip will be as long as the fabric is wide, usually 42" to 44". Divide the fabric width by the cut width of the segments to determine the number of segments you can cut from the strip set.

Now put on your warm-up suit and try the following exercises:

Exercise 1

Suppose you want to make a 6" x 6" Four Patch block, with each square measuring 3" x 3" when finished. Add ½" to the finished size of each square for seam allowances. Therefore, you'll need to cut the strips 3½" wide. Sew the strips into a strip set and cut each segment 3½" wide (the finished size of each square, plus ½"). If your strips are 42" long, you can cut 12 segments, each 3½" wide, from the strip set (42" ÷ 3½" = 12 segments).

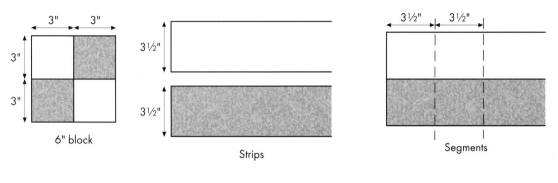

6" block

Strips

Segments

Exercise 2

What if you want the same Four Patch block to measure 5" x 5" finished? Divide 5" by 2 (the number of squares in each row) to arrive at the finished square size of 2½" x 2½". Add ½" to that measurement for seam allowances. Therefore, you'll need to cut the strips 3" wide. Sew the strips into a strip set and cut the segments 3" wide. You can cut 14 segments, each 3" wide, from the strip set (42" ÷ 3" = 14 segments).

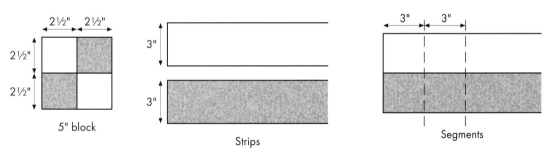

5" block

Strips

Segments

Exercise 3

Now try the same exercise with a Nine Patch block. You fill in the blanks:

For 6" blocks:
Finished size of each small square: 6" ÷ 3 (the number of small squares in each row) = _____.

Cut width of strips: finished size + ½" = _____

Cut width of segments: finished size + ½"= _____

Number of segments: 42" ÷ 2½" = _____

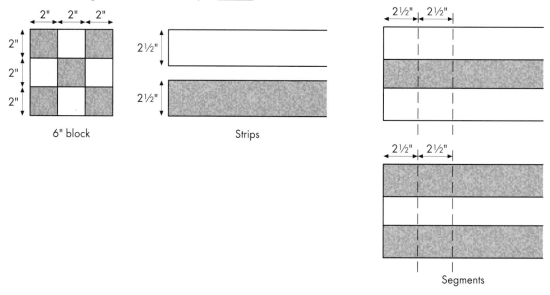

6" block   Strips   Segments

For 9" blocks:
Finished size of each small square:
9" ÷ 3 = _____

Cut width of strips: finished size + ½" = _____

Cut width of segments: finished size +½" = _____

Number of segments: 42" ÷ 3½" = _____

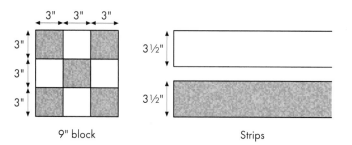

9" block   Strips   Segments

Exercise 4

Now consider a Puss-in-the-Corner block. This block is an uneven Nine Patch made up of squares and rectangles, all connected by straight seams.

See the illustration below for the cut width of the strips and segments for 8" blocks.

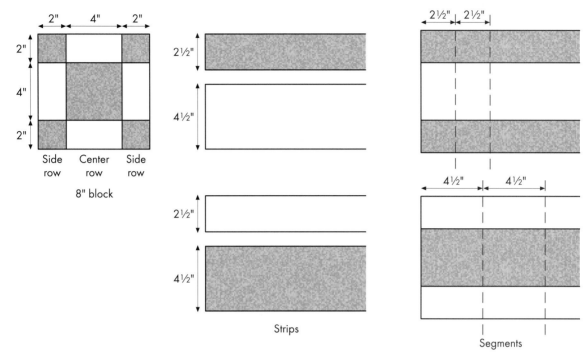

Side row — Center row — Side row

8" block

Strips

Segments

For 6" blocks:

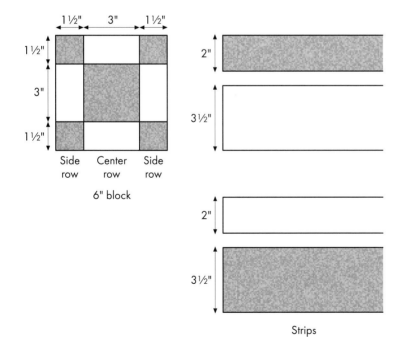

Side row — Center row — Side row

6" block

Strips

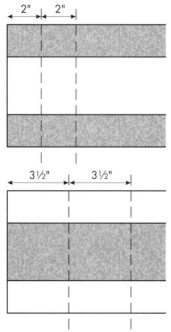

Segments

Exercise 5

Next, work through the numbers for a 6" Rail Fence block:

Finished width of each strip: 6" ÷ 3 (number of strips) = 2"

Cut width of strips: finished size + ½" = 2½"

Cut width of segments: finished size of block + ½" = 6½"

Number of blocks: 42" ÷ 6½" = 6

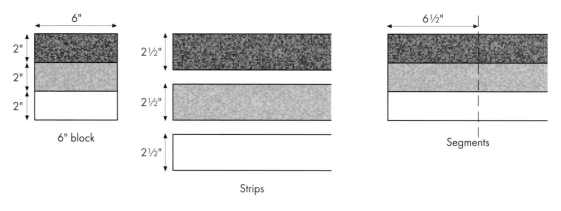

6" block

Strips

Segments

For 3" blocks:

Finished width of each strip: 3" ÷ 3 (number of strips) = _____

Cut width of strips: finished size + ½" = _____

Cut width of segments: finished size of block + ½" = _____

Number of blocks: 42" ÷ 3½" = _____

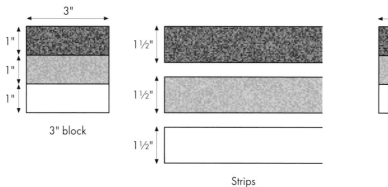

3" block

Strips

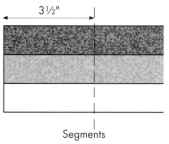

Segments

You can use strip-pieced units in combinations to make other blocks, such as Shoo Fly, Churn Dash, and Jacob's Ladder. Start with strip-pieced elements; then add other parts.

Shoo Fly

Cut the center row, which consists of three squares, from a strip set and make the corner elements as bias squares (page 20). The only other pieces needed are squares for the side rows. Refer to the illustration below to see how to cut the strips, segments, squares, and bias squares for a 6" block.

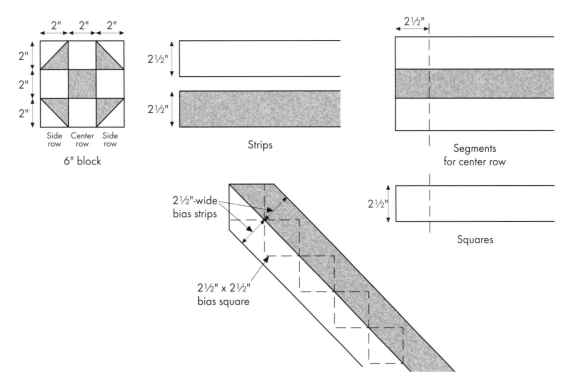

Churn Dash

Strip piece the rectangles and make bias squares for the corners, as in the Shoo Fly block above. Assemble the block with a center square. The illustration below shows the elements needed for an 8" block.

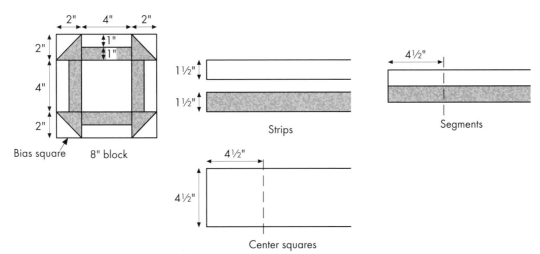

Jacob's Ladder

Combine strip-pieced four-patch units and bias squares to make this traditional block. Let's work through the numbers for a 9" block:

1. Divide 9" by 3 for the finished size of each unit, 3" x 3".
2. For each four-patch unit, divide 3" by 2 for the finished size of each small square, 1½" x 1½". Add ½" for the cut width of the strips (2"). Sew the strips together and cut the segments 2" wide. You can cut 21 segments from each strip set. Re-sew the segments into four-patch units.
3. For the bias squares, which also finish to 3" x 3", cut the strips 3" wide and follow the directions for bias squares on page 20.

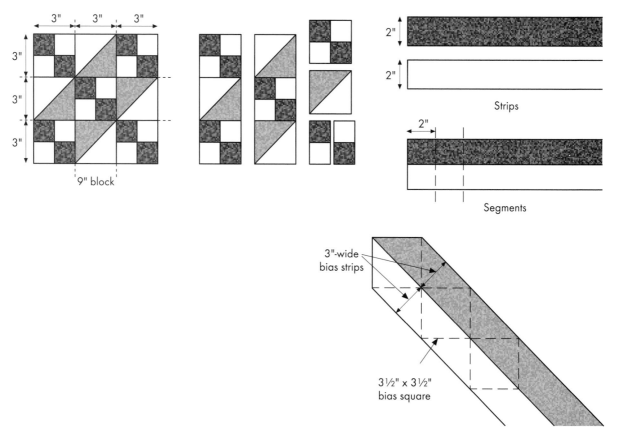

Borders

When it comes to borders for the projects in this book, you have several options: borders with straight-cut corners, borders with corner squares, and strip-pieced borders and sashing.

Cut your border strips across the width of the fabric from selvage to selvage. The projects specify border-strip lengths, but be sure to measure your quilt top through the center before you cut the strips. Your quilt may vary slightly from mine because everyone pieces a little differently.

Borders with Straight-Cut Corners

1. Cut border strips the width specified in the project directions.
2. Measure the length of the quilt top through the center. Cut 2 borders to that length.

3. Pin each side border to the quilt top at the ends and several places in between.
4. Stitch the borders to the sides of the quilt top. Use a square ruler to make sure the corners are square; trim if necessary. Press the borders away from the quilt top.
5. Measure the width of the quilt through the center, including the side borders you just added. Cut 2 borders to that length.

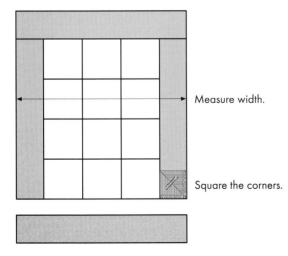

Measure width.

Square the corners.

6. Add the borders to the top and bottom of the quilt top. Square the corners if necessary.

Borders with Corner Squares

1. Cut the border strips the width specified in the project directions. Cut the corner squares the specified size.
2. Measure the length of the quilt top through the center. Cut 2 borders to that length.
3. Measure the width of the quilt top through the center. Cut 2 borders to that length.
4. Follow steps 3 and 4 of "Borders with Straight-Cut Corners," at left, to add the side borders.
5. Stitch a corner square to each end of the top and bottom borders. Press the seams away from the corner squares.
6. Stitch the borders to the top and bottom of the quilt top, matching the corner-square seams with the side-border seams. Press the seams away from the quilt.

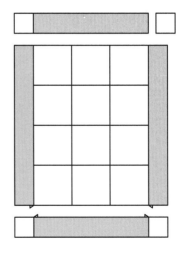

Strip-Pieced Borders and Sashing

Now let's look at ways to use strip-piecing techniques in borders and sashing.

Multiple Borders with Corner Squares

Suppose you want to add a 1" blue border and a 2" white border, with 3" x 3" blue corner squares, to a quilt top that measures 18" x 22".

1. Cut 2 blue strips, each 1½" x the width of the fabric. Cut 2 white strips, each 2½" x the width of the fabric.

2. Join the strips to make 2 strip sets. Add ½" to each quilt-top measurement to determine the length of each border segment. In this example, cut one segment 18½" long and another 22½" long from each strip set. You'll also need to cut 4 blue corner squares, each 3½" x 3½".

3. Add the 22½"-long border strips to the sides of the quilt top. Add the corner squares to the 18½"-long border strips; add these strips to the top and bottom of the quilt top.

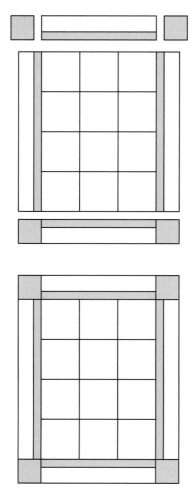

Sashing

There's no need to cut rectangles and squares for sashing; strip piece them instead.

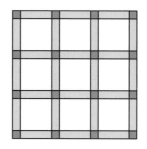

1. Measure the quilt block, including seam allowances, and cut a strip that width. For example, to make a 2"-wide finished sashing on an 8" finished block, cut a strip 8½" wide. From that strip, cut 2½"-wide segments, one for each block. Sew a sashing strip to one side of each block.

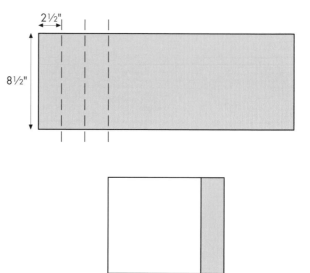

2. Cut a strip 2½" wide for the sashing squares. Add this strip to the remainder of the first strip. Crosscut the strip set into 2½"-wide segments. Join the blocks and segments as shown below. You'll need one additional square, 2½" x 2½", to complete the sashing in the lower left corner.

Here's another great strip-pieced sashing, consisting of two-strip segments and four-patch units. Cut the strips the finished strip width + ½". Cut the sashing segments the finished block size + ½". Cut the four-patch segments the finished width + ½". Alternate the segments when you assemble the quilt top.

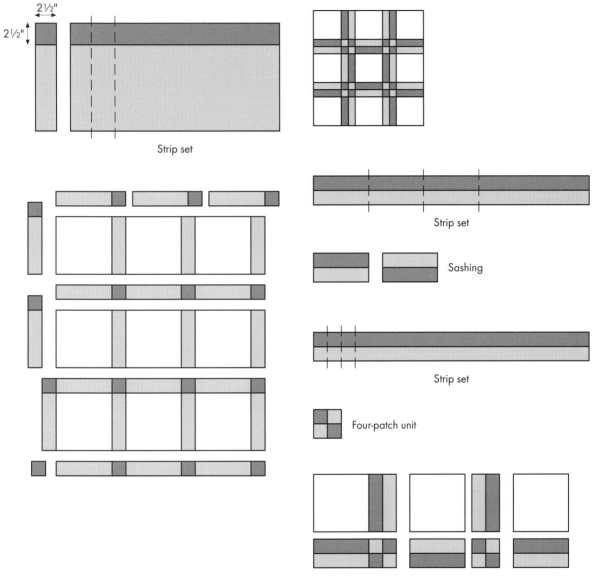

Strip set

Strip set

Sashing

Strip set

Four-patch unit

Sashing and four-patch units

Making Borders Longer

Use a diagonal seam to piece a border; it is stronger and less noticeable than a straight seam.

1. Cut the border strips, making sure the ends are exactly square.

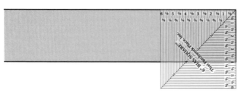

2. Place one border strip, right side up, on the cutting mat. Place another border strip, right side down, with the squared edges aligned.

Exactly square

3. Mark a 45° angle as shown. Pin the strips and stitch on the marked line. Press the seam to the side and trim the excess fabric.

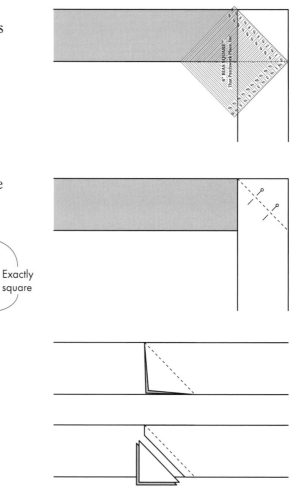

4. Place the seam in an inconspicuous spot on the border, not at the center or near the end. Measure and cut the border from the pieced strip.

Final Touches

Refer to *Your First Quilt Book* for easy instructions on preparing the backing, basting, quilting, and binding, and for making a sleeve to hang your quilt.

Don't forget to add a label to the quilt. You'll be glad to have the information when you've made many beautiful quilts and you want to see where it all started.

Gallery

Four Patch Pillow *by Paulette Peters, 1997, Elkhorn, Nebraska, 16" x 16".*
Strip piece Four Patch blocks, then rotate them in a simple setting for a
flowerlike effect. A pillow is good practice before tackling larger projects.

Table Runner *by Paulette Peters, 1997, Elkhorn, Nebraska,*
18¾" x 40". Trip Around the World, a traditional favorite with quilters,
lends itself to a long, narrow version, just right for the table.

Holiday Wreath *by Paulette Peters, 1997, Elkhorn, Nebraska, 24" x 24".*
Make this simple strip-pieced project for a splash of seasonal
color, or to go under a punch bowl.

Hot Squares *by Paulette Peters, 1997, Elkhorn, Nebraska, 34" x 34".*
Warm colors and strip piecing make a "cool" quilt!

Strip Stripes *by Paulette Peters, 1997, Elkhorn, Nebraska, 35½" x 35½".*
This is only one of many possible settings for these versatile
Roman Stripes blocks. Play with them to create your own design.

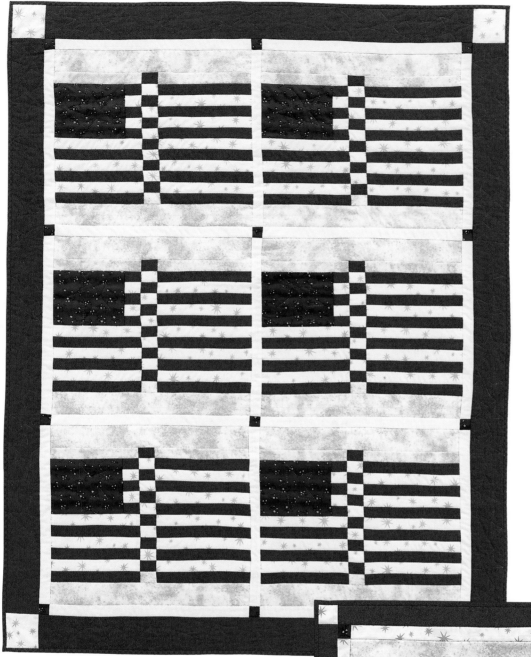

Six Flags *by Paulette Peters, 1997, Elkhorn, Nebraska, 45" x 58". Six flags make for more of a good thing.*

Betsy's Vision *by Paulette Peters, 1997, Elkhorn, Nebraska, 23" x 21". Here's one way to get the flag "flying." One strip-pieced flag is the perfect size for a small wall hanging.*

Blue Shoo Fly *by Paulette Peters, 1997, Elkhorn, Nebraska, 42" x 52".*
Shoo Fly is another traditional block that likes to be strip pieced.
Use four different blues for a scrappy look.

Plaid *by Paulette Peters, 1997, Elkhorn, Nebraska, 32" x 32".*
Visual layers appear when you separate simple blocks with bold sashing strips.
It looks like a plaid—a little loud, but cheerful.

Strip-Piecing Projects

Are you ready to put your new strip-piecing skills to work? On the following pages you'll find eight simple strip-piecing projects. Before you choose a project, read the instructions carefully and look at the illustrations. Some projects, such as "Hot Squares" (page 56), couldn't be easier. Others, like "Plaid" (page 70) and "Blue Shoo Fly" (page 75), are a bit more challenging. You might like to make one of the simpler projects just to get your feet wet, then tackle the more involved ones.

Each set of instructions begins with an illustration and project information, followed by a list of materials. The cutting charts show at a glance how to cut the strips and other pieces you'll need to make your project. If the cutting chart does not specify a minimum strip length, cut the strips across the entire width of the fabric, from selvage to selvage.

It's helpful to sketch a cutting strategy, showing all the pieces required, to make the best use of the yardage.

Step-by-step instructions will guide you through each stage of construction. Pay careful attention to the pressing instructions and the one-sided pressing arrows; properly pressed seam allowances are essential to successful strip piecing.

The instructions in the "Borders" section of each project tell you how long to trim the border strips. These are "perfect measurements," meaning they are mathematically correct. In reality, your project will vary slightly, so be sure to measure your assembled patchwork before you trim the border strips.

If you need help finishing your project (layering, quilting, binding, and labeling), refer to *Your First Quilt Book*. I have included a quilting suggestion with each project, but feel free to create your own design.

Four Patch Pillow

A Four Patch pillow is a great starter project if you're new to strip piecing. Make many, and you'll soon have a "plethora of pillows."

Project Information at a Glance	
Finished Pillow Size: 16" x 16"	
Name of Block: Four Patch	
Finished Block Size: 13½" x 13½"	
Number of Blocks: 1	
Finished Border Width: 1¼"	

Materials: 44"-wide fabric

½ yd. cream or muslin for blocks and pillow top backing

⅝ yd. green batik for center square, borders, and pillow back

⅛ yd. or fat quarter of light rose for blocks

¼ yd. or fat quarter of dark rose for blocks

18" x 18" square of low-loft batting

16" pillow form

Choosing Fabric

Select two fabrics in flower colors and surround them with green to suggest nature. Look for different prints and textures in your fabrics. Mix large-scale, widely spaced prints with small-scale, dense ones and a multicolored green batik.

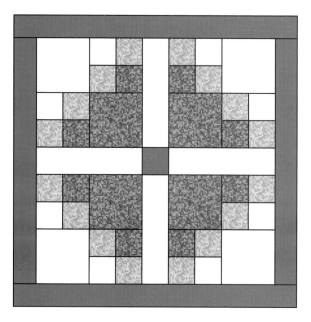

Color photo on page 33.

Cutting

All measurements include ¼"-wide seam allowances.

1. Cut a square, 18" x 18", from the cream fabric or muslin and set it aside to back the pillow top for quilting.

2. Cut 2 rectangles, each 14" x 17", from the green fabric and set them aside for the back of the pillow.

Cut the strips from selvage to selvage across the width of the fabric.

 Green

 Light rose

 Dark rose

 Cream

Fabric	Cut Width	No. of Strips	Minimum Length	Piece	Placement
Cream	2"	1	17"		Strip sets
	2"	2	14"	4 rectangles, each 2" x 6½"	C
	3½"	1	15"	4 squares, each 3½" x 3½"	A
Green	2"	2	36"	1 square, 2" x 2"	Borders D
Light rose	2"	2	17"		Strip sets
Dark rose	2"	1	17"		Strip sets
	3½"	1	15"	4 squares, each 3½" x 3½"	B

Strip Sets

1. For Strip Set 1, join a light rose strip and a cream strip.

2. For Strip Set 2, join a light rose strip and a dark rose strip.

Four Patches

1. Lay Strip Set 1, right side up, on your cutting mat. Lay Strip Set 2, right side down, on Strip Set 1 as shown. (Be sure that the two light rose strips aren't on top of each other.) Run your finger along the seams, smoothing them so they interlock. Cut 8 segments, each 2" wide, cutting through both strip sets at the same time.

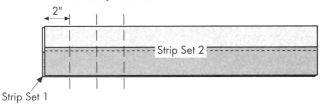

2. With a pair of segments still together, stitch using a ¼"-wide seam allowance. Chain-piece the remaining pairs.

3. Press the seams to one side. Now you have 8 little four-patch units, each 3½" x 3½".

Make 8.

Pillow Assembly

1. Join 1 cream square (Piece A) to the side of a four-patch unit as shown.

2. Join 1 dark rose square (Piece B) to the side of a four-patch unit as shown.

3. Join the units.

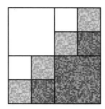

Make 4.

4. Join 2 units from step 3 and a cream rectangle (Piece C) to make a row.

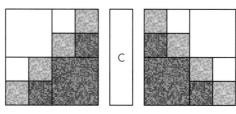

Make 2.

5. Join 2 cream rectangles (Piece C) and the green square (Piece D).

6. Join the rows to complete the block.

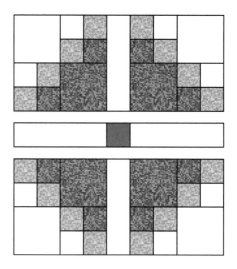

Borders

1. From the green strips, trim 2 side borders, each 2" x 14". Trim the top and bottom borders, each 2" x 17".

2. Add the borders. (See "Borders with Straight-Cut Corners" on page 29.)

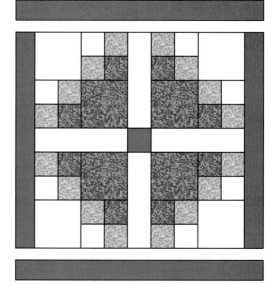

Quilting

1. Layer the pillow top with batting and backing; baste.
2. Quilt as desired.
3. Baste ¼" from the edge to keep the borders and corners square. Trim the excess batting and backing.

Finishing

1. On each 14" x 17" green rectangle, turn under ¼" on one long edge. Turn under another 1½" and machine stitch.

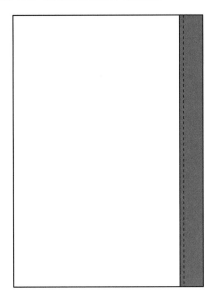

2. With right sides together, place one hemmed rectangle on the quilted pillow top, matching the outside edges. Baste ¼" from the edges.

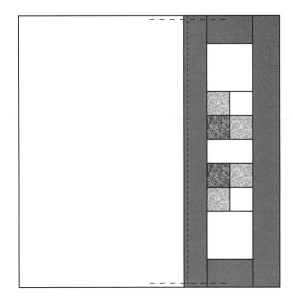

3. Place the other rectangle on the pillow top, right sides together; pin. Stitch through all layers, using a ½"-wide seam allowance; double stitch where the rectangles overlap.

4. Trim the batting from the seam allowances. Trim the corners and turn the pillow right side out. Pop in the pillow form.

To taper the corners so they don't form exaggerated points, follow these steps:

1. Prepare the pillow top and pillow back pieces for finishing.
2. On each edge of the pillow top, make a mark 4" from each corner. Also make a mark ½" from each corner.
3. Connect the marks with a ruler and a pencil. This will be your cutting line.
4. Start stitching at the midpoint of any edge. As you near each corner, stitch ½" from the marked line. Cut on the line.

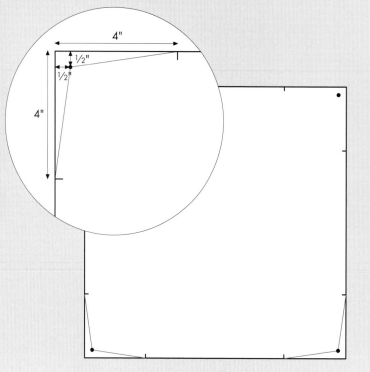

Table Runner

This pattern sews so quickly, you'll want to make several for gifts, or one for each season. You can make the runner longer by adding rows. Each row adds approximately 4¼" to the length.

Project Information at a Glance

Finished Runner Size: 18¾" x 40"

Name of Block: Trip Around the World

Finished Inner Border Width: 1"

Finished Outer Border Width: 2"

Materials: 44"-wide fabric

⅛ yd. yellow for patchwork

1⅛ yds. multicolored print on white for patchwork, outer border, and lining (back of runner)

½ yd. blue for patchwork

¼ yd. bright green for inner border

⅔ yd. muslin for backing

23" x 44" piece of batting

Note: Use a very flat batting.

 White print

 Yellow

 Blue

Green

Color photo on page 34.

Choosing Fabric

I started with the white print and chose colors from there. The yellow and green are bright and clear; for contrast, the blue is more muted.

For this table runner, I used a blue plaid that required careful attention to grain lines. I recommend using a print until you're more experienced with strip piecing. If you wish to use a plaid, choose a small-scale, symmetrical plaid and cut the strips for the strip sets on the true bias. (See "Making Bias Squares" on page 20 to cut bias strips.) Cut the yellow and the white strips crosswise, from selvage to selvage. Follow the directions, taking care not to stretch the blue strips. The plaid will run in the same direction in the squares and the edge triangles, and the straight grain will be on the edges.

Cutting

All measurements include ¼"-wide seam allowances.

Cut the strips from selvage to selvage across the width of the fabric.

Fabric	Cut Width	No. of Strips	Segments	Second Cut	Placement
Yellow	3½"	1	3½"		Strip sets
White print	3½"	2	3½"		Strip sets
	From each white print strip, cut 2 squares, each 3½" x 3½" (4 total).				
	2½"	3			Outer border
Blue	3½"	2	3½"		Strip sets
	5½"	1	5 squares, each 5½" x 5½"	⊠	20 edge triangles Use 18.
			2 squares, each 3½" x 3½"	⧄	4 corner triangles
Green	1½"	3			Inner border

⊠ Cut the squares twice diagonally.   ⧄ Cut the squares once diagonally.

Strip Sets

1. Join a 3½"-wide white strip to a 3½"-wide blue strip to make a pair. Make a second pair. Press the seam allowances toward the blue strips. Cut 1 segment, 3½" wide, from each pair. Set these segments aside for step 3 in "Table Runner Assembly."

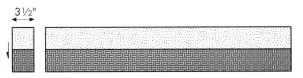

3½"

2. Sew the blue/white strip pairs to each side of the yellow strip, with blue touching yellow. Press the seam allowances toward the blue strips. From this strip set, cut 6 segments, each 3½" wide.

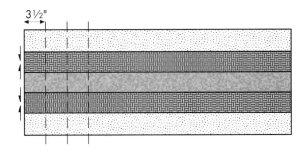

3½"

Table Runner Assembly

1. Sew a blue triangle to one end of 2 segments cut in step 2, above. Start sewing at the right angle of the triangle, not at the tip. Set these rows aside.

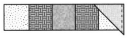

Make 2.

2. Sew a blue triangle to each end of 4 segments. Set these rows aside.

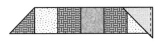

Make 4.

3. Assemble 2 corner units as follows:

    Sew a blue triangle to 2 opposite sides of a white square.

    Sew a white square to a blue/white pair you set aside in step 1 of "Strip Sets."

    Sew a blue triangle to each end of the unit you just made.

    Join the units to make a corner unit. Make an additional corner unit.

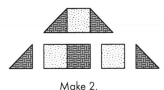

Make 2.

4. Pin the rows together at the intersections, offsetting the squares. The rows without a triangle at one end should be on opposite ends of the piece.

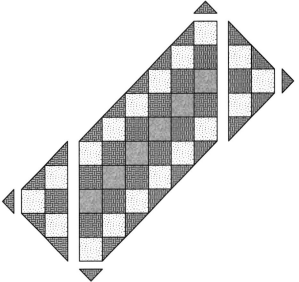

Note: The triangles are a little larger than necessary. Match the intersection of the squares and let the points of the triangles extend beyond the squares.

If you are sewing a blue square to a blue square, you're not offsetting the rows.

5. Start stitching where the triangles overlap to form a V. The needle will drop in right at the ¼"-wide seam allowance.

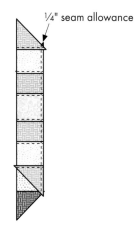

¼" seam allowance

6. Sew a corner unit to each end of the runner.
7. Add the 4 corner triangles. These will be slightly larger than necessary. Use your rotary equipment to trim them to a square corner.

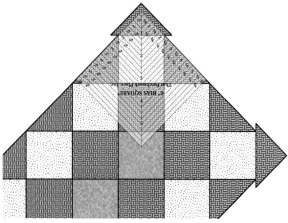

8. Press the seams. Trim the dog ears off the triangles.

Borders

Be sure to measure the patchwork before trimming the border strips.

1. From the green strips, trim 2 side borders, each 1½" x 34½". Trim 2 end borders, each 1½" x 15¼".
2. From the 2½"-wide white strips, trim 2 side borders, each 2½" x 36½". Trim 2 end borders, each 2½" x 19¼".
3. Add the side green borders, then the end green borders. Repeat for the white borders. (See "Borders with Straight-Cut Corners" on page 29.)

Finishing

See *Your First Quilt Book* for complete directions. Your table runner will lie flatter if it doesn't have a binding. Here's how to make an "envelope" lining.

1. Layer the runner with muslin backing and batting; baste.
2. Quilt by hand or machine. See the quilting suggestion below.

3. Machine baste ¼" from the edge of the runner. Trim the batting and backing even with the top.

4. Cut 2 pieces of white print, each 19¼" x 24". Turn under ¼" on one short edge of one piece; press. Lay the piece right side down on half of the quilted runner; pin.

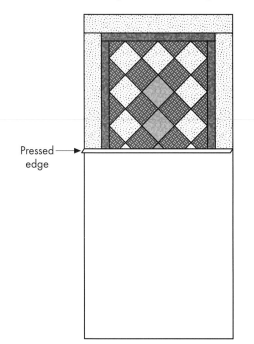

Pressed edge

5. Lay the other piece, right side down, on the runner, overlapping the pressed edge; pin.

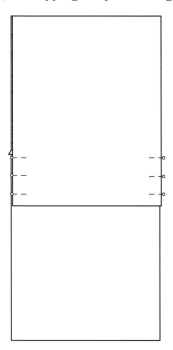

6. Stitch around the edges, using a walking foot and a generous ¼"-wide seam allowance.

7. Trim the lining. Trim the corners at a right angle.

8. Turn the runner right side out and push out the seams and corners. Lightly press the edges. Hand stitch the pressed edge closed.

9. Machine or hand quilt through all layers on the inside edge of the inner border.

Holiday Wreath

Make four strip-pieced blocks and rotate them to create a festive wreath. This project is so quick that you'll want to make a wreath for every season. Replace the red with fall leaf colors, or use spring greens with pink or yellow. Place your wreath under a table centerpiece or add a bow and display it on the wall.

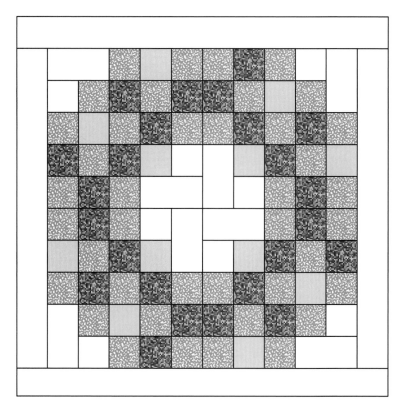

Color photo on page 35.

Project Information at a Glance
Finished Quilt Size: 24" x 24"
Finished Block Size: 10" x 10"
Number of Blocks: 4
Finished Border Width: 2"

Materials: 44"-wide fabric or fat quarters

¼ yd. or fat quarter of light green
¼ yd. or fat quarter of dark green
⅛ yd. or fat quarter of red
½ yd. white
¾ yd. for backing
Add ¼ yd. to one of the above fabrics for binding.
28" x 28" piece of batting
1½ yds. of wire-edged ribbon, 1½" wide (optional)

Choosing Fabric

Pick greens with extra colors in their prints for visual texture. Use a large-scale print for one green and a smaller-scale print for the other.

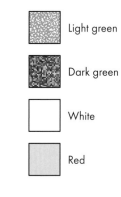

Light green

Dark green

White

Red

Cutting

All measurements include ¼"-wide seam allowances.

Cut each strip 10½" long, across the width of the fabric. You can cut 4 strips from fabric that has 42" of usable width. You can cut 2 strips from the long (22") side of a fat quarter. Cut the border strips after you have assembled and joined the blocks.

Fabric	Cut Width	No. of Strips (44" fabric)	No. of Strips (fat quarters)	No. of 10½" Lengths	Placement
Light green	2½"	3	5	10	Strip sets
Dark green	2½"	2	3	6	Strip sets
Red	2½"	1	2	3	Strip sets
White	4½"	1	–	2	Strip sets
	2½"	1	–	2	Strip sets
	2½"	3	–	–	Borders
Binding	2½"	3	–	–	

Strip Sets

1. Each row of the block requires a strip set that is 10½" long. Make 5 strip sets, one for each row, as shown at right. Press the seams in Strip Sets 1, 3, and 5 to the left. Press the seams in Strip Sets 2 and 4 to the right. Mark each strip set with a numbered piece of masking tape.

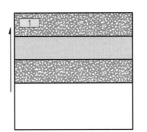

Strip Set 1

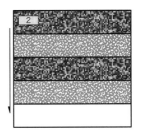

Strip Set 2

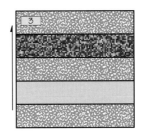

Strip Set 3

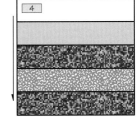

Strip Set 4

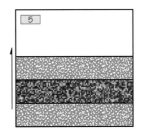

Strip Set 5

2. Cut each strip set into 4 segments, each 2½"
wide. Keep your segments organized by
placing the segments from each strip set in
little stacks of 4.

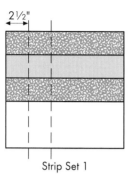

Strip Set 1

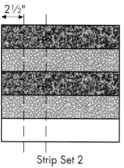

Strip Set 2

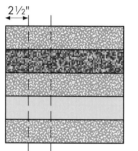

Strip Set 3

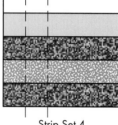

Strip Set 4

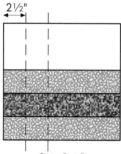

Strip Set 5

Wreath Assembly

1. Arrange the rows as shown. Put a pin in the
upper left corner of each row to help you remember which is the left edge. Sew the rows
together, matching the seam intersections.
Make 4 blocks. Press the seams toward Row 5.

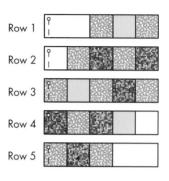

Row 1
Row 2
Row 3
Row 4
Row 5

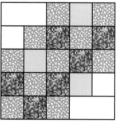

Make 4.

2. Place a pin in the upper left corner of each
block. Lay out the blocks as shown below,
rotating each one clockwise. Double-check
the placement. Is there a red square in each
corner of the center?

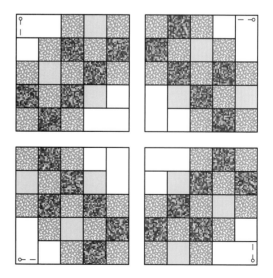

3. Join the blocks, matching the intersections.

Borders

1. Cut 2 side borders, each 2½" x 20½", from 1 white border strip. Cut the top and bottom borders, each 2½" x 24½", from the remaining 2 strips.
2. Add the borders. (See "Borders with Straight-Cut Corners" on page 29.)

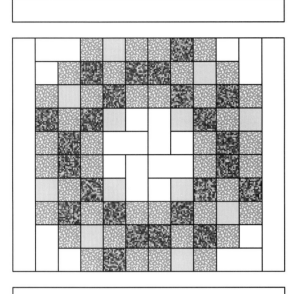

Finishing

See *Your First Quilt Book* for complete finishing directions.

1. Layer the quilt top with batting and backing; baste.
2. Quilt by hand or machine. See the quilting suggestion below.

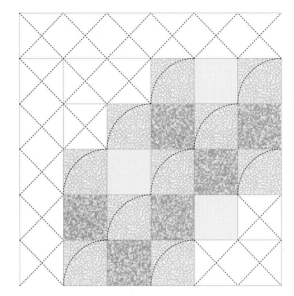

3. Bind the edges with 2½"-wide strips of your chosen fabric.
4. Optional: Tie the ribbon like a shoelace. Pouf the bow into a pleasing shape and safety-pin in place.
5. Add a label to your quilt.

Hot Squares

Alternate Four Patch and Nine Patch blocks to make squares of color that dance across the quilt surface. It's fast and fun!

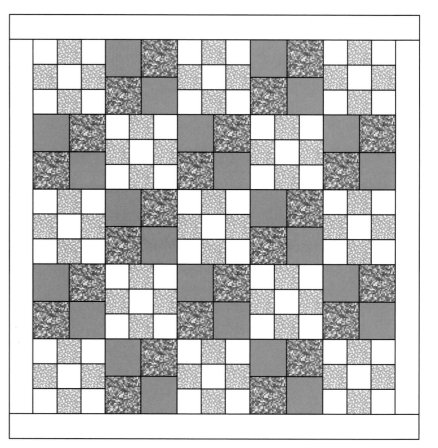

Color photo on page 36.

Project Information at a Glance		
Finished Quilt Size: 34" x 34"		
Name of Block:	Four Patch	Nine Patch
Finished Block Size:	6" x 6"	6" x 6"
Number of Blocks:	12	13
Finished Border Width: 2"		

Materials: 44"-wide fabric

¼ yd. blue batik for blocks
⅝ yd. fuchsia for blocks and binding
⅓ yd. mauve for blocks
¾ yd. cream for blocks and border
1 yd. fabric for backing
36" x 36" piece of batting

Choosing Fabric

For the Four Patch blocks, choose a dark value and a medium value. I used a dark hot fuchsia and a medium blue batik. For the Nine Patch blocks, choose a light value and a medium value. I chose a cream and a mauve.

 Batik

Fuchsia

Mauve

 Cream

Cutting

All measurements include ¼"-wide seam allowances.

Cut the strips from selvage to selvage across the width of the fabric.

Note: For the Four Patch blocks, your fabrics must have a little more than 42" of usable width to allow you to cut 12 segments, each 3½" wide.

Fabric	Cut Width	No. of Strips	Minimum Length	Segments	Placement
Blue batik	3½"	2	42"+	3½"	4-patch strip sets
Fuchsia	3½"	2	42"+	3½"	4-patch strip sets
	2½"	4			Binding
Mauve	2½"	4	36"	2½"	9-patch strip sets
Cream	2½"	5	36"	2½"	9-patch strip sets
	2½"	4	36"		Borders

Layer the two fabrics for each block combination, right sides together, and cut the strips. Now they're ready to sew. If you use a batik for the Four Patch blocks, double-check the right side; it can be difficult to identify.

Four Patch Blocks

Strip Sets

1. Sew a batik strip to a fuchsia strip to make a strip set. Make an additional strip set. Press the seam allowance toward the dark fabric.

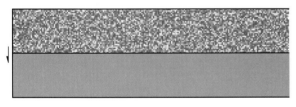

Make 2.

2. Lay a strip set on the cutting mat, right side up, with a horizontal edge on a grid line. Lay the other strip set on the first one, right side down. Make sure the same colors are not on top of each other. Run your finger over the seam, nestling the intersections snugly so the seams interlock.

3. Check the alignment on the mat. Is the long edge of the strip set aligned with the horizontal grid line? Trim the rough edges. Cut 12 segments, each 3½" wide.

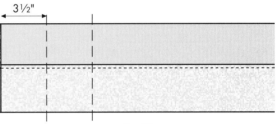

3½"

Cut 12.

Trim sparingly. There is very little room for error in this strip set.

Block Assembly

Leaving the paired segments together, chain-piece them to make 12 blocks. Press the seam allowances to one side.

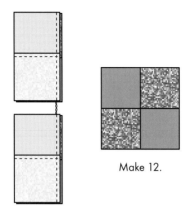

Make 12.

Nine Patch Blocks

Strip Sets

1. Sew a mauve strip to a cream strip to make a strip set. Make a total of 3 strip sets. Press the seam allowances toward the dark fabric.

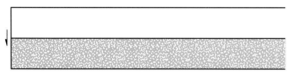

Make 3.

2. Add an extra white strip to each of 2 strip sets, and an extra mauve strip to the remaining strip set. Press the seam allowances toward the dark fabric.

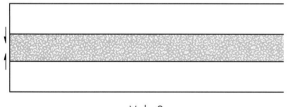

Make 2.

Make 1.

3. Align the strip sets as you did for the Four Patch blocks, with the seams interlocking. Check the alignment on the mat. Are the long edges of the strip sets aligned with a horizontal grid line? Align the markings on your ruler with the grid line and trim the rough edges. Cut 13 segments, each 2½" wide. Leave the pairs together.

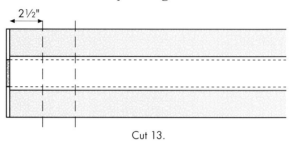

2½"

Cut 13.

4. Cut 13 segments, each 2½" wide, from the remaining strip set.

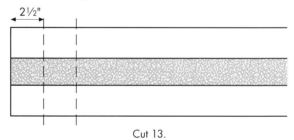

2½"

Cut 13.

Block Assembly

1. Chain-piece the paired segments. Sew slowly, checking the seam intersections as you go.

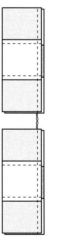
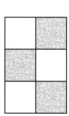

2. Chain-piece the units made in the previous step and the remaining segments, matching the seam intersections. Press the seam allowances away from the center.

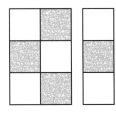

 Your blocks should measure 6½" x 6½". If the Four Patch blocks are a little larger than the Nine Patch blocks, recheck the seam guide on your machine before your next project. If you must trim the Four Patch blocks, trim them on all four sides to keep the seam intersection in the center of the block.

Quilt Assembly

1. Arrange the blocks in a checkerboard pattern, with a Nine Patch block in each corner. Arrange the Four Patch blocks so they form diagonal lines of dark squares.

2. Sew the blocks together in rows. Press the seams in Rows 1, 3, and 5 to the left. Press the seams in Rows 2 and 4 to the right. Join the rows.

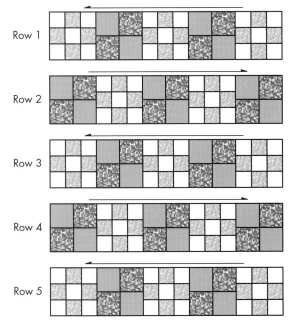

Borders

1. Trim 2 side border strips, each 2½" x 30½". Trim the top and bottom border strips, each 2½" x 34½".

2. Add the borders. (See "Borders with Straight-Cut Corners" on page 29.)

Finishing

See *Your First Quilt Book* for complete finishing directions.

1. Layer the quilt top with batting and backing; baste.

2. Quilt by hand or machine. See the quilting suggestion below.

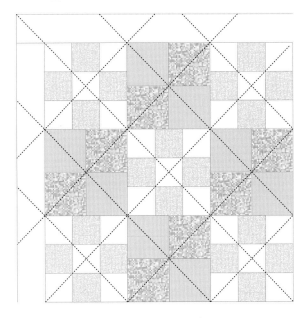

3. Bind the edges with the fuchsia strips.

4. Add a label to your quilt.

Strip Stripes

This simple quilt consists of traditional Roman Stripes blocks in a symmetrical setting. You see this block often in Amish quilts, and it's just as beautiful in today's fabrics.

Color photo on page 37.

Project Information at a Glance

Finished Quilt Size: 35½" x 35½"

Name of Block: Roman Stripes

Finished Block Size: 7⅛" x 7⅛"

Number of Blocks with Floral Triangles: 4

Number of Blocks with White Triangles: 12

Finished Border Width: 3½"

Materials: 44"-wide fabric

⅜ yd. purple for blocks

⅜ yd. fuchsia for blocks

⅜ yd. green for blocks

¼ yd. gold for blocks

½ yd. white for blocks

1⅛ yds. multicolored print for blocks, border, and binding

1⅛ yds. fabric for backing

40" x 40" piece of batting

Choosing Fabric

Start with a multicolored print, such as the floral border fabric in this quilt. Select a contrasting background fabric that is plain or tone-on-tone. I used white-on-white for my background. You could choose a softer background, such as pale yellow, blue, or gray. Just be sure there is enough contrast between the background and the other fabrics to see the block design.

Use four colors from the print for the stripes. Look for fabrics with varying textures and values, and arrange them for maximum contrast.

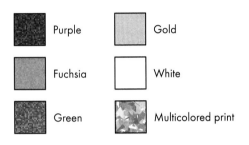

■	Purple	▨	Gold
▦	Fuchsia	□	White
▨	Green	▧	Multicolored print

Cutting

All measurements include ¼"-wide seam allowances.

Cut strips from selvage to selvage across the width of the fabric. Cut the border strips after you have assembled and joined the blocks.

Fabric	Cut Width	No. of Strips	Segments	Second Cut	Placement
Purple	1¾"	6			Strip sets
Fuchsia	1¾"	6			Strip sets

Note: Layer the purple and fuchsia fabrics, right sides together, and cut at the same time. Your pairs will be ready to sew.

Fabric	Cut Width	No. of Strips	Segments	Second Cut	Placement
Green	1¾"	6			Strip sets
Gold	2½"	3			Strip sets
White	8"	2	6 squares, each 8" x 8"	◩	12 triangles
Multicolored print	8"	1	2 squares, each 8" x 8"	◩	4 triangles
	4"	4			Borders
	2½"	4			Binding

◩ Cut the squares once diagonally.

Strip Sets

1. Sew the purple and fuchsia strips together into 6 pairs. In 3 pairs, press the seam allowances toward the fuchsia. In the other 3 pairs, press the seam allowances toward the purple.

Make 3.

Make 3.

2. Sew a green strip to the fuchsia side of all 6 pairs. Press the seams in the same direction on each set.

Make 3.

Make 3.

3. Divide the sets into 2 piles, according to the direction of the seam allowances. Sew a set from each pile to a gold strip, with the green touching the gold. Press all seam allowances on the strip set in the same direction. Make 3 strip sets.

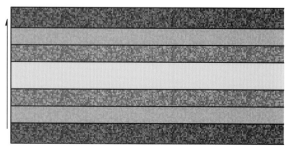

Make 3.

Each strip set should have a purple strip on each outside edge.

Block Assembly

1. Lay 2 multicolored triangles along one edge of a strip set, matching the raw edges. Repeat on the opposite edge of the strip set. You may need to shift the triangles until they all fit, and you will have leftover areas in the center of the strip set. Pin the triangles and the strip set on the long edges.

Multicolored triangles

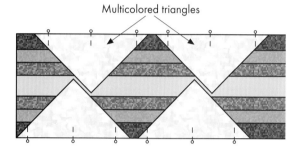

2. Sew along both edges, using a ¼"-wide seam allowance.
3. Place a square ruler along the edges of each triangle as shown and cut through the strip set.
4. Repeat on the remaining 2 strip sets, using the white triangles.

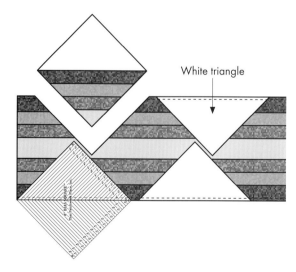

White triangle

5. Press the seams in the same direction as the strips in each block. Your blocks are finished.

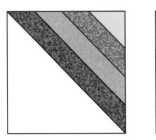 

Make 12. Make 4.

Quilt Assembly

Arrange the blocks as shown below. Sew the blocks together in sets of 4; then sew the sets together.

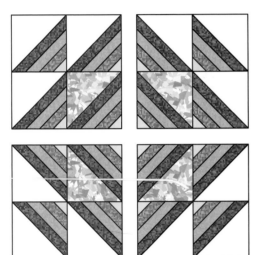

 The seams in half of the blocks are pressed toward the plain triangles. Arrange them so they are next to blocks with seams pressed away from the triangles. It will be easier to match the seams.

Borders

1. Trim 2 side border strips, each 4" x 29". Trim the top and bottom border strips, each 4" x 36".
2. Add the borders. (See "Borders with Straight-Cut Corners" on page 29.)

Finishing

See *Your First Quilt Book* for complete finishing directions.

1. Layer the quilt top with batting and backing; baste.
2. Quilt by hand or machine. See the quilting suggestion below.

3. Bind the edges with the multicolored print strips.
4. Add a label to your quilt.

Betsy's Vision

Betsy Ross, that is. Don't you think she would have loved strip piecing? If only she had owned a rotary cutter! This folk-art flag has fewer stripes than Betsy's. It's fun to make for patriotic friends.

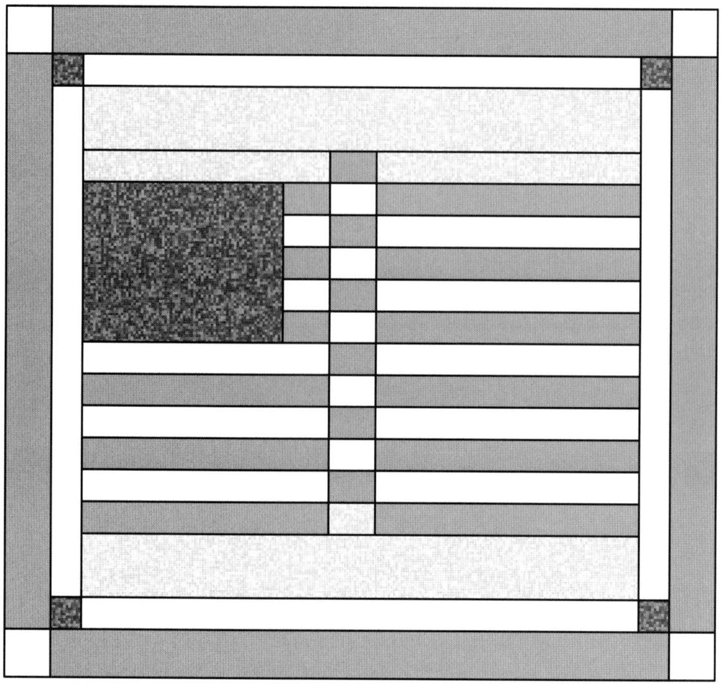

Color photo on page 38.

Project Information at a Glance
Finished Quilt Size (one flag): 23" x 21"
Finished Border Widths: 1" and 1½"
Finished Quilt Size (six flags): 45" x 58"
Finished Sashing Width: 1"
Finished Border Width: 3"
Finished Block Size: 16" x 18"

Materials: 44"-wide fabric

	One Flag	Six Flags
Red	⅝ yd.	1⅞ yds.
White	⅜ yd.	1⅜ yds.
Flag blue	¼ yd.	⅜ yd.
Sky blue	¼ yd.	¾ yd.
Backing	¾ yd.	2⅔ yds.
Batting	27" x 25"	49" x 62"

Choosing Fabric

Have fun with these fabrics. "Flag blue" can be bright or navy, and it doesn't need to have stars. Look for a print with a white design on navy. The red and white stripes can be prints or plain fabrics. Choose a light blue that says "sky" for the sky fabric.

Note: Red dyes in fabrics often bleed. Prewash the fabrics, and make sure the red fabric is colorfast.

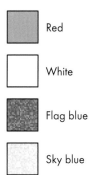

Red

White

Flag blue

Sky blue

Cutting

All measurements include ¼"-wide seam allowances.

Note: Following are directions for one flag. I prefer to work with one flag at a time because each flag grows from one long strip set. Following the instructions for the one-flag quilt, you'll find instructions for the sashing and borders on the six-flag quilt.

Cut strips from selvage to selvage across the width of the fabric.

Fabric	Cut Width	No. of Strips	Minimum Length	Segments
Red	1½"	3	42"	Strip set
White	1½"	3	42"	Strip set
Flag blue	5½"	1	8"	1 rectangle, 5½" x 7"
Sky blue	1½"	1	42"	1 rectangle, 1½" x 8½" Use remainder of strip in "Strip Sets," step 5.
	2½"	1	38"	2 strips, each 2½" x 18½"

Strip Sets

 There are many strips to manage; use special care to press the strip sets straight and flat with no creases or pleats.

1. Make 1 strip set using 3 red strips and 2 white strips. Press the seams toward the red strips. The strip set should measure 5½" wide.

2. Cut 1 segment, 2" wide, from the strip set. Sew the segment to the right edge of the flag-blue rectangle.

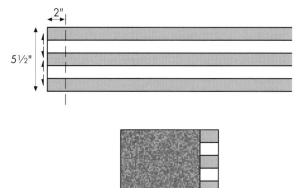

3. Cut the strip set in half to make 2 partial strip sets.

4. Add a white strip to one of the partial strip sets. Press the seam toward the red strip. This strip set should measure 6½" wide. Cut a segment, 6½" x 8½", from the strip set.

Sew the white edge of the segment to the bottom of the flag-blue rectangle unit made in step 2. Sew the 1½" x 8½" sky-blue rectangle to the top of the unit. Whew! The left side of the block is done.

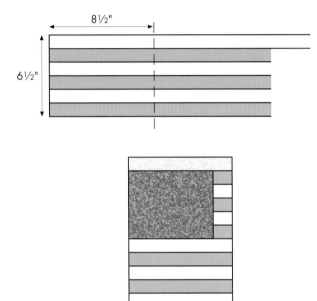

5. Sew the remaining pieces of the partial strip sets together. Add the remainder of the 1½"-wide sky-blue strip to the lower red edge of the strip set. Press the seam toward the red strip. The strip set should measure 12½" wide.

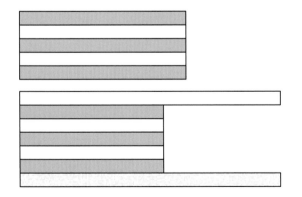

6. Cut a segment, 2" x 12½", from the strip set. Position the segment so the sky-blue strip is at the bottom. Also cut a segment, 9" x 12½". Turn it so the sky-blue strip is at the top. Join the segments, with the smaller piece on the left.

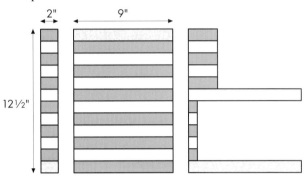

7. Join the left and right sides of the block, matching the seam intersections. Aren't you glad you pressed all the seams toward the red strips?

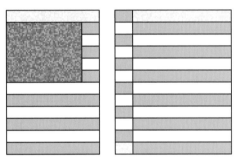

8. Add a sky-blue strip, 2½" x 18½", to the top and bottom of the block.

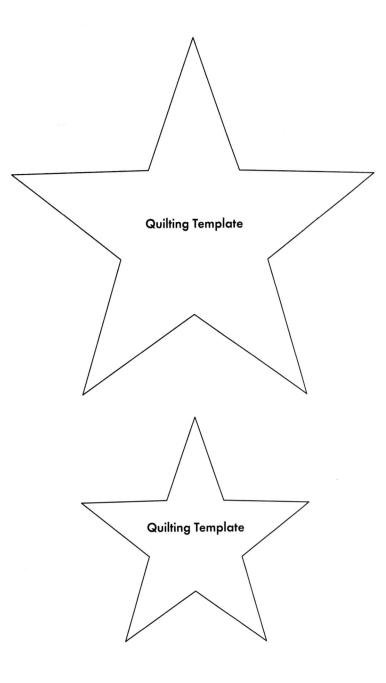

Quilting Template

Quilting Template

Plaid

Sashing frames nine blocks in this simple quilt, creating the effect of a plaid. Practice making bias squares in the Sawtooth border.

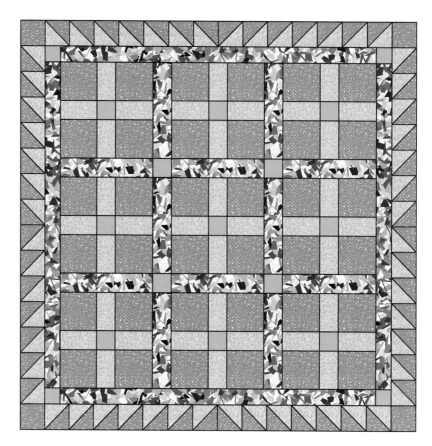

Color photo on page 40.

Project Information at a Glance

Finished Quilt Size: 32" x 32"

Name of Block: Nine Patch Variation

Finished Block Size: 7½" x 7½"

Number of Blocks: 9

Finished Sashing Width: 1½"

Finished First Border Width: 1¼"

Finished Sawtooth Border Width: 2"

Materials: 44"-wide fabric

1¼ yds. teal for blocks, Sawtooth border, and binding

⅞ yd. gold for blocks and Sawtooth border

⅛ yd. red for blocks and corner squares

½ yd. black print for sashing and first border

1 yd. fabric for backing

36" x 36" piece of batting

Choosing Fabric

Have fun with these colors! To create a grid effect, as if the quilt has visual layers, choose fabrics with plenty of contrast.

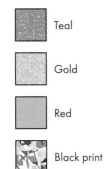

Teal

Gold

Red

Black print

Cutting

All measurements include ¼"-wide seam allowances.

Cut strips from selvage to selvage across the width of the fabric. Cut the black print border strips after you assemble and join the blocks and sashing.

Fabric	Cut Width	No. of Strips	Size	Placement
Teal	3½"	3		Strip sets
	18" square			Sawtooth border bias squares
	2½"	4		Binding
	4 squares, each 2½" x 2½"			Sawtooth border corners
Gold	2"	2		Strip sets
	3½"	1		Strip sets
	18" square			Sawtooth border bias squares
Red	2"	1	2" x 22"	Strip set
			2" x 10"	Sashing
	4 squares, each 1¾" x 1¾"			First border corners
Black print	8"	1		Sashing
	1¾"	4		First border

Strip Sets

1. Make 1 full-length strip set and 1 half-length strip set as follows: Sew a 3½"-wide teal strip to each edge of a 2"-wide gold strip. Cut the remaining teal strip in half; sew a half strip to each edge of a 2"-wide gold strip. Press the seams toward the teal strips. Cut 18 segments, each 3½" wide.

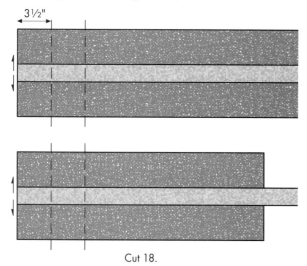

Cut 18.

2. Cut the 3½"-wide gold strip in half. Sew a half gold strip to each edge of the 22"-long red strip. Press the seams toward the red strip. Cut 9 segments, each 2" wide.

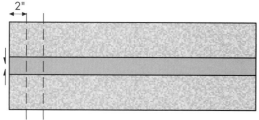

Cut 9.

Block Assembly

Join the segments to make 1 block. Make 9 blocks.

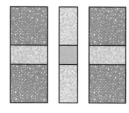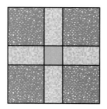

Make 9.

Sashing

1. Cut 8 sashing pieces, each 2" x 8", from the 8"-wide black print strip. Sew a segment to one edge of 6 blocks.

Cut 8.

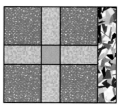

Make 6.

It's important to line up the gold strips in the blocks, even though the blocks are separated by sashing. Before pressing each sashing strip away from the block, use a ruler to mark where the gold strip in the next block should join the sashing strip. When you join the blocks, match the marks to the seams of the gold strip.

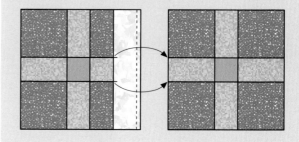

2. Sew the 10"-long red strip to the remaining black print strip. Cut 4 segments, each 2" wide.

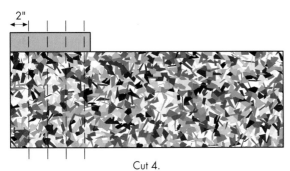

Cut 4.

Quilt Assembly

Assemble the blocks and sashing strips into rows. Join the rows.

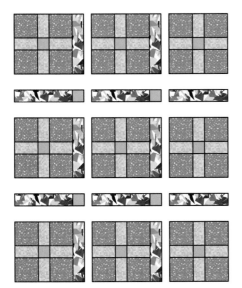

Borders

First Border

1. From the 1¾"-wide black print strips, trim 4 borders, each 1¾" x 26".
2. Add the black print border with red corner squares. (See "Borders with Corner Squares" on page 29.)

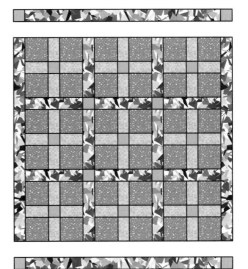

Second Border

See "Making Bias Squares" on pages 20–21 for complete instructions.

1. Layer the 18" teal square and 18" gold square, right sides together, matching the lengthwise grain. Cut bias strips, each 2½" wide.

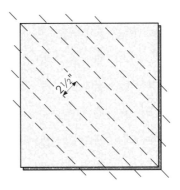

2. Using Method 1 or Method 2, make 56 bias squares, each 2½" x 2½".

3. Make 4 borders of 14 bias squares each, with the bias squares turned as shown.

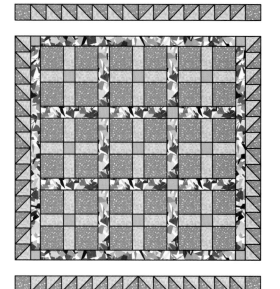

4. Add the Sawtooth side borders. Join the 2½" teal corner squares to the ends of the top and bottom Sawtooth borders and add to the quilt top.

Finishing

See *Your First Quilt Book* for complete finishing directions.

1. Layer the quilt top with batting and backing; baste.
2. Quilt by hand or machine. Quilt in-the-ditch of each piece, or quilt as desired.
3. Bind the edges with the teal strips.
4. Add a label to your quilt.

Blue Shoo Fly

Twelve Shoo Fly blocks, set on point, make a quilt big enough to snuggle under. Repeat the Shoo Fly pattern for a simple quilting design in the setting pieces.

Color photo on page 39.

Project Information at a Glance

Finished Quilt Size: 42" x 52"

Name of Block: Shoo Fly

Finished Block Size: 7½" x 7½"

Number of Blocks: 12

Finished Border Width: 5"

Materials: 44"-wide fabric

1⅞ yds. white print for blocks and borders

1⅜ yds. main blue print for 3 blocks, setting pieces, and binding

3 fat quarters of blue prints for blocks

1⅝ yds. fabric for backing

46" x 56" piece of batting

Choosing Fabric

Use one white print for the block background and four medium-to–dark blue prints for the blocks. Make sure there is good contrast between the white print and each blue print. Pick your favorite blue for the setting pieces and binding.

☐ White print

■ Main blue print

■ Blue print 1

▨ Blue print 2

▨ Blue print 3

Cutting

All measurements include ¼"-wide seam allowances.

Cut strips from selvage to selvage across the width of the fabric.

Fabric	Cut Width	No. of Strips	Piece	Second Cut	Placement
White print	3½"	2	24 rectangles, each 2" x 3½"		Blocks
	3½"	2			Strip sets
	12"	2	4 squares, each 12" x 12"		Bias strips
	5½"	4			Borders
Main blue print	2"	1			Strip sets
	12"	1	3 squares, each 12" x 12"	⊠	12 side setting triangles Use 10.
			1 square, 12" x 12"		Bias strips
			6 squares, each 8" x 8"		Setting squares
			2 squares, each 6¼" x 6¼"	⊡	Corner setting triangles
	2½"	5			Binding
3 blue fat quarters			1 square, 12" x 12", from each		Bias strips
From one of the blues			4 squares, each 5½" x 5½"		Border corners

⊠ Cut the squares twice diagonally.   ⊡ Cut the squares once diagonally.

Strip Sets

1. Sew a 3½"-wide white strip to each edge of the 2"-wide blue strip. Press the seams toward the white print.
2. Cut 12 segments, each 2" wide, for the centers of the blocks.

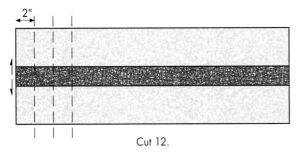

Cut 12.

Bias Squares

1. Layer a 12" white square and a 12" blue square, right sides together, matching the lengthwise grain. Cut bias strips, each 3" wide.

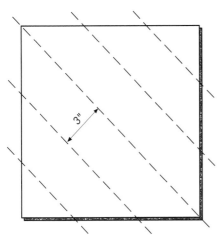

2. Using Method 1 or Method 2 on page 21, make 12 bias squares, each 3½" x 3½".
3. Repeat steps 1 and 2 with the other 12" blue squares and 12" white squares to make a total of 48 bias squares.

4. Assemble 12 blocks, using matching bias squares, the center segments from the strip sets, and 2 each of the 2" x 3½" rectangles.

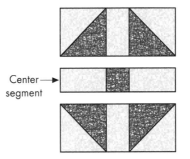

Center segment →

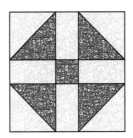

Make 3 from each blue fabric.

Quilt Assembly

Arrange the blocks in diagonal rows of same-color blocks with blue setting squares and side setting triangles. Join the blocks, setting squares, and side setting triangles into rows; join the rows. Add the corner setting triangles.

Borders

1. From the 5½"-wide white strips, trim 4 border strips to the proper lengths. (See "Borders with Corner Squares" on page 29.)
2. Add the white borders with blue corner squares.

Finishing

See *Your First Quilt Book* for complete finishing directions.

1. Layer the quilt top with batting and backing; baste.
2. Outline quilt each block and setting square. See the quilting suggestion below.

3. Bind the edges with the blue strips.
4. Add a label to your quilt.

Meet the Author

A Nebraska quiltmaker and teacher, Paulette is past president of the Nebraska State Quilt Guild and serves on NSQG's Quilt Preservation Project steering committee. She is a co-founder of Cottonwood Quilters of Nebraska.

She has written two books, *Corners in the Cabin* and *Borders by Design*, published by That Patchwork Place.

Paulette teaches and lectures across the country, and her work has been widely published. Some of these publications include *Rotary Riot* and *Make Room for Quilts*, published by That Patchwork Place; *Quilter's Newsletter Magazine*; and *Nebraska Quilts and Quiltmakers*, published by the University of Nebraska Press.

She and her husband, Terry, have a married daughter, two married sons, and a one-year-old granddaughter, who already has her first of many quilts.

Bibliography

Doak, Carol. *Your First Quilt Book*. Bothell, Wash.: That Patchwork Place, Inc., 1997.

Martin, Nancy J. *Back to Square One*. Bothell, Wash.: That Patchwork Place, Inc., 1988.

Thomas, Donna Lynn. *Shortcuts: A Concise Guide to Rotary Cutting*. Bothell, Wash.: That Patchwork Place, Inc., 1991.

Books from
Martingale & Company

That Patchwork Place • FIBER STUDIO PRESS • Pastimes

Appliqué

Appliquilt® Your ABCs
Baltimore Bouquets
Basic Quiltmaking Techniques for Hand Appliqué
Coxcomb Quilt
The Easy Art of Appliqué
Folk Art Animals
From a Quilter's Garden
Stars in the Garden
Sunbonnet Sue All Through the Year
Traditional Blocks Meet Appliqué
Welcome to the North Pole

Borders and Bindings

Borders by Design
The Border Workbook
A Fine Finish
Happy Endings
Interlacing Borders
Traditional Quilts with Painless Borders

Design Reference

All New! Copy Art for Quilters
Blockbender Quilts
Color: The Quilter's Guide
Design Essentials: The Quilter's Guide
Design Your Own Quilts
Freedom in Design
The Log Cabin Design Workbook
The Nature of Design
QuiltSkills
Sensational Settings
Surprising Designs from Traditional Quilt Blocks

Foundation/Paper Piecing

Classic Quilts with Precise Foundation Piecing
Crazy but Pieceable
Easy Machine Paper Piecing
Easy Mix & Match Machine Paper Piecing
Easy Paper-Pieced Keepsake Quilts
Easy Paper-Pieced Miniatures
Easy Reversible Vests
Go Wild with Quilts
Go Wild with Quilts—Again!
A Quilter's Ark
Show Me How to Paper Piece

Hand and Machine Quilting/Stitching

Loving Stitches
Machine Needlelace and Other
    Embellishment Techniques
Machine Quilting Made Easy
Machine Quilting with Decorative Threads
Quilting Design Sourcebook
Quilting Makes the Quilt
Thread Magic
Threadplay with Libby Lehman

Home Decorating

Decorate with Quilts & Collections
The Home Decorator's Stamping Book
Living with Little Quilts
Make Room for Quilts
Soft Furnishings for Your Home
Welcome Home: Debbie Mumm

Miniature/Small Quilts

Beyond Charm Quilts
Celebrate! with Little Quilts
Easy Paper-Pieced Miniatures
Fun with Miniature Log Cabin Blocks
Little Quilts All Through the House
Lively Little Logs
Living with Little Quilts
Miniature Baltimore Album Quilts
No Big Deal
A Silk-Ribbon Album
Small Talk

Needle Arts/Ribbonry

Christmas Ribbonry
Crazy Rags
Hand-Stitched Samplers from I Done My Best
Miniature Baltimore Album Quilts
A Passion for Ribbonry
A Silk-Ribbon Album
Victorian Elegance

Quiltmaking Basics

Basic Quiltmaking Techniques for Hand Appliqué
Basic Quiltmaking Techniques for Strip Piecing
The Joy of Quilting
A Perfect Match
Press for Success
The Ultimate Book of Quilt Labels
Your First Quilt Book (or it should be!)

Rotary Cutting/Speed Piecing

Around the Block with Judy Hopkins
All-Star Sampler
Bargello Quilts
Block by Block
Down the Rotary Road with Judy Hopkins
Easy Star Sampler
Magic Base Blocks for Unlimited Quilt Designs
A New Slant on Bargello Quilts
Quilting Up a Storm
Rotary Riot
Rotary Roundup
ScrapMania
Simply Scrappy Quilts
Square Dance
Stripples
Stripples Strikes Again!
Strips that Sizzle
Two-Color Quilts

Seasonal Quilts

Appliquilt® for Christmas
Christmas Ribbonry
Easy Seasonal Wall Quilts
Folded Fabric Fun
Quilted for Christmas
Quilted for Christmas, Book II
Quilted for Christmas, Book III
Quilted for Christmas, Book IV
Welcome to the North Pole

Surface Design/Fabric Manipulation

15 Beads: A Guide to Creating One-of-a-Kind Beads
The Art of Handmade Paper and Collage
Complex Cloth: A Comprehensive Guide
    to Surface Design
Dyes & Paints: A Hands-On Guide to Coloring Fabric
Hand-Dyed Fabric Made Easy

Theme Quilts

The Cat's Meow
Celebrating the Quilt
Class-Act Quilts
The Heirloom Quilt
Honoring the Seasons
Kids Can Quilt
Life in the Country with Country Threads
Lora & Company
Making Memories
More Quilts for Baby
Once Upon a Quilt
Patchwork Pantry
Quick-Sew Celebrations
Quilted Landscapes
Quilted Legends of the West
Quilts: An American Legacy
Quilts for Baby
Quilts from Nature
Through the Window and Beyond

Watercolor Quilts

Awash with Colour
More Strip-Pieced Watercolor Magic
Strip-Pieced Watercolor Magic
Watercolor Impressions
Watercolor Quilts

Wearables

Crazy Rags
Dress Daze
Dressed by the Best
Easy Reversible Vests
More Jazz from Judy Murrah
Quick-Sew Fleece
Sew a Work of Art Inside and Out
Variations in Chenille

Many of these books are available through your local quilt, fabric, craft-supply, or art-supply store. For more information, call, write, fax, or e-mail for our free full-color catalog.

Martingale & Company
PO Box 118
Bothell, WA 98041-0118 USA

1-800-426-3126
International: 1-425-483-3313
24-Hour Fax: 1-425-486-7596
Web site: www.patchwork.com
E-mail: info@patchwork.com

11/98